Amrit Kaal Odyssey

Amrit Kaal Odyssey

100 Strides for Viksit Bharat@100

Rangam Trivedi • Vaidyanathan Iyer

Published by
PRABHAT PRAKASHAN PVT. LTD.
4/19 Asaf Ali Road,
New Delhi-110 002 (INDIA)
e-mail: prabhatbooks@gmail.com

ISBN 978-93-5521-935-0
AMRIT KAAL ODYSSEY
by Shri Rangam Trivedi & Shri Vaidyanathan Iyer

Edition
First, 2024

Paperback Price
₹ 499.00 (Rupees Four Hundred Ninety Nine only)

Printed at
R-Tech Offset Printers, Delhi

Foreword

Prime Minister Narendra Modiji has transformed Bharat in last 10 years. This transformation is visible across all the sectors, be it railways, highways, healthcare, education, etc.

'Amrit Kaal Odyssey' captures the 100 most impactful such transformations. It shows the commitment of Prime Minister Modi's vision of *Sabka Sath, Sabka Vikas, Sabka Vishwas* and *Sabka Prayas*. The former will help readers, particularly young readers to easily understand the impact of this transformation.

As we enter our Amrit kaal, this book will help us understand our achievements and plans for Viksit Bharat. Congratulations to the authors for their commendable efforts.

—Ashwini Vaishnaw
Union Minister for Railways,
Electronics & IT, and Communications

Preface

In the tapestry of Bharat's rich history, the thread of governance intricately weaves through the ages, resonating from the 'Vidya Sabha' and 'Raj Sabha' in the ancient *'Yajurveda'* to the profound wisdom embedded in the *'Brihadaranya Upanishad'*. This sacred land, illuminated by the ideals of 'Ram Rajya' and Kautilya's *'Arthshastra'* has long embraced the essence of effective governance.

The last decade, a transformative epoch since 2014, marked the dawn of a new era in governance. From shedding the tag of the 'fragile five' to ascending the pinnacle as the 'fastest-growing' economy globally, Bharat embarked on a journey towards self-reliance, emerging as the *'vishwa mitra'*. Notably, 248 million people were uplifted out of multidimensional poverty in the past decade. The multi-sectoral statistical data provides tangible evidence of growth that forms the pillars of 'Viksit Bharat' ushering in 'Amrit Kaal'.

In the past decade, Bharat embraced the mantra of 'reform, perform and transform', laying a robust grassroots foundation. Notable feats range from the Statue of Unity to the world's tallest, and the Chenab Bridge, the highest rail-bridge. Initiatives like 'Jal Jeevan Mission' and 'Namami Gange' prioritise water and Ganga restoration. The National War Memorial honours heroes and the Padma Awards celebrate change-makers. From 180+ nations that participated in World Yoga Day to Prime Minister Narendra Modi recognised as 'The Boss' by global leaders – these signify Bharat's evolution as a developed nation.

A decade ago, India grappled with misgovernance. People's welfare suffered, the economy faltered, global reputation waned and infrastructure development lagged. The nation thirsted for development. Post-2014, a transformative era dawned, marking progress, development and renewed optimism for India's future where the nation is taking a new shape, fulfilling the aspirations of its youth, empowering the women to lead, prospering the farmers, modernising the villages and uplifting the poor.

Coined by Prime Minister Narendra Modi during the 75th Independence Day address, the concept of 'Amrit Kaal' symbolises a pivotal juncture. As the nation charts the course towards a 'Viksit Bharat', setting new global benchmarks, this book meticulously unfolds 100 impactful initiatives across 20 major sectors by the Government of India in the past decade. These initiatives, now integral to the nation's fabric, act as catalysts that propel Bharat towards the status of a developed nation at its centenary of Independence.

Transitioning from voluminous texts to a harmonious blend of precise data-rich research, eloquent literary expressions and captivating artistic illustrations, this book promises a unique reading experience for enthusiasts of public policies and governance.

What sets this book apart is its resonance with the perspectives and ideals of the youth, envisioning 'Viksit Bharat' during the 'Amrit Kaal'. The passionate narrative and exquisite illustrations make it an invaluable resource for young researchers, civil services aspirants and students preparing for competitive exams and job interviews.

An embodiment of strengthened democracy in the 'Amrit Kaal', this book signifies a paradigm shift. What was once a subject evoking disinterest among the youth has now become an avenue for learning about the evolution of their country – the largest democracy and the cradle of democracy – now hailed as the global capital of good governance.

With a mission to inform, inspire and involve the '*amrit*

peedhi' in the marvels of governance, this book stands as a beacon, fostering research in governance and public policy. It is an earnest effort to kindle the flame of motivation and engagement, beckoning the youth to join the glorious journey towards 'Viksit Bharat@2047'.

Acknowledgements

We wish to express our profound gratitude to the talented artists who have illuminated the 100 initiatives with their digital sketch art—Dhruvi Jain, Chinank Pasricha, Anshul Gupta, and Sophie Almaz. Our heartfelt appreciation goes to the Kanti Rana Hobby Centre, Vadodara, for facilitating the connection with these young artists. We also extend our thanks to the Niravadya Foundation for their invaluable support in providing the policy sketches featured in this book.

We are immensely thankful to the Honourable Union Minister for Railways, Electronics & IT, and Communications, Government of Bharat Shri Ashwini Vaishnaw, for graciously commending our efforts through his foreword.

We are also grateful to BlueKraft Digital Foundation for supporting us in this journey.

Contents

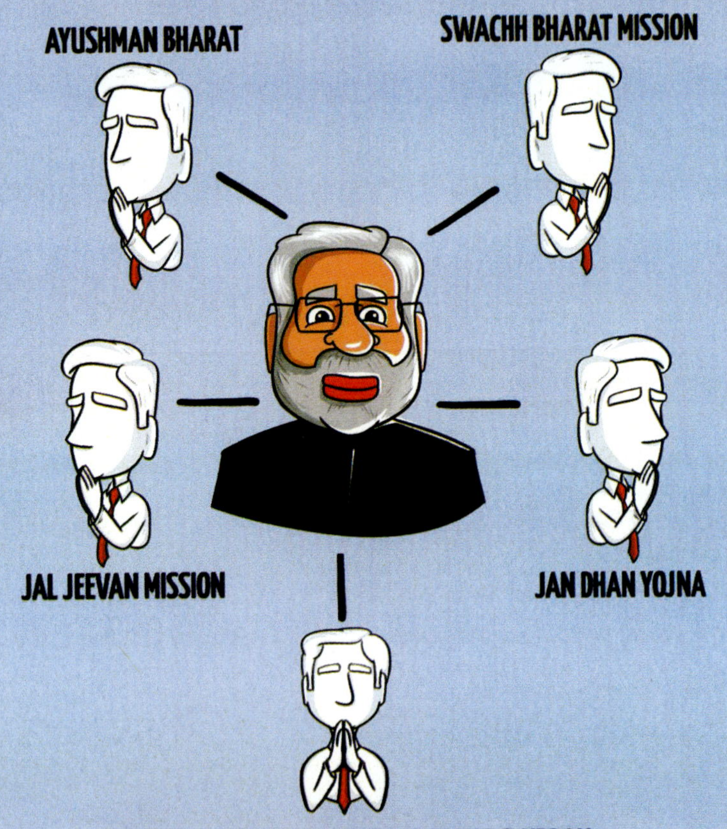
GEARING GOVERNANCE
AYUSHMAN BHARAT
SWACHH BHARAT MISSION
JAL JEEVAN MISSION
JAN DHAN YOJNA
PRADHAN MANTRI AWAS YOJNA RURAL & URBAN
Anshul Gupta

Section-1

Gearing Governance

"At the core of good governance is service delivery at the grassroots level. In 'Amrit Kaal', we remain resolute in our efforts towards making a positive impact in people's lives and creating a developed India."

—Prime Minister Shri Narendra Modi
(Independence Day address, Red Fort,
New Delhi, on 15.08.2021)

HOSPITAL
15,000+
PRIVATE & GOVERNMENT
HOSPITALS.
30.55+ CRORE
AYUSHMAN BHARAT
CARDS HAVE BEEN
ISSUED.
AS OF JANUARY 2024.
AYUSHMAN BHARAT
CARD
₹. 5,00,000
HEALT
INSURANCE
INCLUDES
1393
MEDICAL
PROCEDURE.

1. PMJAY: A Beacon of Health Transformation

Bharat has transcended an era where severe illnesses financially devastated families in lower-income groups. The Ayushman Bharat – Pradhan Mantri Jan Arogya Yojna (PMJAY) stands as the world's most extensive government-funded health assurance scheme. The provision of free health coverage up to ₹5 lakhs for secondary and tertiary treatments, a reality since 2018, has positively impacted over 50 crore citizens. This figure is equivalent to the total population of countries like Uganda, Spain and Sudan. The scheme has transformed the healthcare landscape, offering unprecedented support and protection to citizens who could have never fathomed such comprehensive health coverage.

- 30.55+ crore Ayushman Bharat cards have been issued and 6+ crore citizens have benefited from free treatment till January 2024 since its launch.
- Not just limited to medicines, this covers free treatment up to ₹5 lakhs and which includes supplies, diagnostic services, physician's fees, room charges, surgeon charges, OT and ICU charges, etc.
- This scheme includes 1,393 medical procedures including critical illness.
- 15,000+ private and government hospitals are empanelled under PMJAY.
- Due to this scheme, poor and lower-income group families have saved around ₹1 lakh crore cumulatively since its launch.

THEN..
NOW...
10.93+ CRORE
NEW HOUSEHOLD
TAP CONNECTIONS
(AUG 2019 - JAN 2024)
9 STATES AND
UT INCLUDED.
SAFE & AFFORDABLE DRINKING WATER

2. Jal Jeevan: Quenching Bharat's Thirst for Progress

No longer will the global photography competitions showcase images of women trekking for kilometres with water-filled pots; Bharat has redefined its narrative. Embracing the mantra of 'ease of living' and commited to providing 100 per cent functional household tap-water connections (FHTC) in rural areas by 2024, the nation has surged from 16.82% to an impressive 73.57% rural tap-water coverage since the initiation of the Jal Jeevan Mission in 2019. This unique mission, engaging local communities through 'Pani Samitis', has left an indelible impact on implementation. Addressing a 72-year-old issue post-Independence, it exemplifies the rapid strides toward 'Viksit Bharat' in 2047, characterising the essence of 'Amrit Kaal'.

- This mission has led to 10.93+ crore household tap-water connections till January 2024 since its launch, taking the total to over 14.17+ crore connections.
- Nine states and UTs including Gujarat, Himachal Pradesh, Telangana, Goa, Punjab and Haryana have already achieved the 100% mark earlier in the year 2023.
- Bharat will achieve the UN SDG 6.1 much earlier in 2024, which aims to achieve universal and equitable access to safe and affordable drinking water for all by 2030.
- This would save 5.5 crore hours each day which are wasted during water collection, especially by women, giving them space to spread their wings of growth.
- This would result in averting almost 4,00,000 diarrhoeal-disease deaths across the country.

WASTE SEGREGATION
WASTE
DRY WASTE
WET WASTE
LAND FILLING
WASTE COLLECTION
SWACHH BHARAT
WASTE PROCESS
11.34+ CRORE TOILETS WERE CONSTRUCTED.
SOLID WASTE MANAGEMENT FACILITIES & LIQUID WASTE MANAGEMENT FACILITIES HAVE BEEN DEVELOPED IN 2.54+ LAKH VILLAGES & 4.15 LAKH VILLAGES RESPECTIVELY.
MAKING 6 LAKH VILLAGES OPEN DEFECATION FREE

3. Swachh Bharat Mission: Sanitary Revolution Unveiled

The pivotal year of 2014 marked the onset of new India's transformative journey, with the Swachh Bharat Mission emerging as a monumental stride, evolving from an initial step into the world's largest sanitation initiative. The mission propelled the country's sanitation coverage from 39% in 2014 to a remarkable 100% in 2019, accomplishing UN SDG 6.2 11 years ahead of schedule. Phase 2, initiated in 2020, aspires to cultivate ODF plus and ODF plus rising villages, encompassing comprehensive solid and liquid waste management for sustainable progress. Beyond sanitation, it resonates in shaping a Swastha Bharat and safeguarding the dignity of women through widespread implementation of 'Izzat Ghar'.

- 11.34+ crore household toilets were constructed across the country, making nearly six lakh villages open defecation-free in a short period of just five years.
- Till November 2023, over 4.84+ lakh villages have been given ODF plus status under Phase 2 with an overall budget outlay of 1.43+ lakh crore rupees.
- Solid waste management facilities and liquid waste management facilities have been developed in 2.54+ lakh villages and 4.15+ lakh villages respectively, till November 2023.
- Phase 2 of SBM includes waste management of biodegradable waste, plastic waste, fecal sludge management, soak pits, compost pits, biogas plants, etc.
- Unsafe sanitation led to 199 million diarrhoea cases annually in India, which were reduced drastically post-2019 due to ODF villages.

NEW BANK ACCOUNTS OPENED IN A WEEK...
INDIA
18,09,613
GUINNESS WORLD RECORDS
RuPay
DEBIT
MOBILE BANKING
BENEFITS
DIRECT BENEFITS TRANSFER
INSURANCES
CREDIT
mudra
GOVERNMENT SCHEMES

4. From Unbanked to Empowered: Jan Dhan's Journey

A forward-looking vision, aiming to realise '*antyodaya*' through the last-mile delivery of government welfare schemes and the financial inclusion of every citizen, is imperative for propelling Bharat into the top three positions on the global economic stage. The Pradhan Mantri Jan Dhan Yojna, initiated in 2014 to ensure financial inclusion, stands as a foundational step in new India's illustrious journey during the 'Amrit Kaal', steering towards the vision of 'Viksit Bharat' by 2047. This transformative scheme empowers the unbanked to establish basic zero-balance savings accounts, fostering financial accessibility with interest on deposits.

- A total of 50.89+ crore bank accounts were opened including 33.98+ crores in rural and semi-urban areas consisting of 28.24+ crore female beneficiaries having ₹2,08,131.99 crore balance in the beneficiaries' accounts in November 2023.
- RuPay debit card and an overdraft facility of up to ₹10,000 to eligible account holders are available under this scheme.
- A Guinness World Record has also recognised this scheme for opening the most bank accounts in a week, i.e. 18,096,130 from 23rd to 29th August 2014.
- Beneficiaries are eligible for all government schemes, such as MUDRA, Direct Benefit Transfer, insurance as well as credit, and remittance.
- Accident Insurance Cover of ₹1 lakh (enhanced to ₹2 lakhs for new PMJDY accounts opened after 28.8.2018) is available with a RuPay card issued to the PMJDY account holders.

1.18+ CRORE HOUSES HAVE BEEN SANCTIONED, 1.13+ CRORE HOUSES GROUNDED AND 79.26+ LAKH HOUSES COMPLETED UNDER PMAY URBAN SCHEME.
2.54+ CRORE HOUSES HAVE BEEN SANCTIONED & 2.49 CRORE HOUSES HAVE BEEN COMPLETED UNDER PMAY RURAL SCHEME SINCE ITS LAUNCH.
HOME OWNER

5. Building Pride: PMAY's Socio-economic Resurgence

The PMAY, both in urban and rural sectors, embodies an unwavering commitment to providing affordable, all-weather *pucca* housing of quality to the economically weaker sections, launched in 2015 and 2016 respectively. Unlike previous government housing schemes with inherent flaws, this initiative prioritises improved construction technology, enhanced monitoring, transparency, amenities and efficient convergence in its swift implementation. This project created 6 crore direct and indirect jobs. Mandating ownership or co-ownership for women, the scheme serves as an empowerment tool. By ensuring dignified living, along with a sense of security and ownership pride, PMAY contributes significantly to the socio-economic empowerment narrative of 'Amrit Kaal'.

- PMAY urban: 79.26+ lakh completed out of 1.18+ crore houses sanctioned, using 24 construction technologies as of January 2024.
- PMAY rural: 2.54+ crore completed out of 2.94+ crore houses sanctioned, promoting affordable housing as of January 2024.
- 70% of the homes are registered in the name of women under this scheme.
- 24 technologies and 33 materials adopted for speedy, sustainable and cost-effective projects in PMAY.
- A robust MIS system ensures seamless management of physical and financial progress in PMAY.

□

SHE LEADS

BETI BACHAO BETI PADHAO & SUKANYA SAMRIDHI YOJNA
NARI SHAKTI VANDAN ADHINIYAM
PERMANENT COMMISSION IN ARMED FORCES
MISSION SHAKTI
ECONOMIC EMPOWERMENT OF WOMEN
Anshul Gupta

Section-2

She Leads

"The most effective way to empower women is through a women-led development approach and Bharat is making huge strides in this direction."

—Prime Minister Shri Narendra Modi
(G20 Ministerial Conference on Women Empowerment, 02.08.2023)

Provoding 33% reservation,
the 'Nari Shakti Vandan Adhiniyam'
grants women members reserved
seats in Loksabha
and state assemblies.

6. Breaking Barriers: Nari Shakti Vandan in Bharat

In a historic stride for women-led development, Bharat achieved a milestone with the passage of the Women's Reservation Bill in September 2023 under the Nari Shakti Vandan Act. This groundbreaking legislation signifies a paradigm shift towards inclusive governance, breaking barriers to women's participation in policy- and law-making. Rooted in Bharatiya *sanskriti*, the Act reflects a monumental moment after 27 years of attempts. The Nari Shakti Vandan Adhiniyam not only signifies a triumph for women but also strengthens democracy, ushering in a more inclusive and developed era through enhanced participation in democratic governance.

- Nari Shakti Vandan Adhiniyam provides 33% reservation for women in Lok Sabha and state assemblies.
- It was the first bill introduced in the newly inaugurated Parliament building.
- The bill suggests a 15-year reservation, with additional quotas for SCs and STs among the allocated seats for women.
- Enactment of the bill will increase women members in Lok Sabha from 82 to 181 (17th Lok Sabha).
- To ensure fairness, seats designated for women will rotate after each delimitation exercise.

Enrolment of girls in secondary education increased
from 75.51% to 79.46 %
2014-15 to 2019-2021

7. Transformative Ode: 'Beti Bachao, Beti Padhao' Impact

Beti Bachao, Beti Padhao (BBBP) scheme, launched in 2015, transcends from being a mere initiative to a transformative ode to valuing the girl child. Amidst concerns of a declining Child Sex Ratio, this endeavour emerges as a beacon, weaving a life-cycle continuum for the empowerment of girls and women. With a symphony of nationwide media campaigns and strategic interventions in 405 districts, BP orchestrates an attitudinal shift, nurturing a society that treasures its daughters. The scheme's initial focus on media advocacy, sown in 2015, bore seeds of awareness and behavioural metamorphosis, birthing a brand with indelible recall – BBBP, an anthem for India's journey towards gender equality and women's empowerment in 'Amrit Kaal'.

- The sex ratio at birth at the national level improved by 15 points from 918 to 933 from 2014-15 to 2022-23.
- Enrolment of girls in secondary education increased from 75.51% to 79.46% from 2014-15 to 2020-21.
- Percentage of 1st trimester ANC registration improved from 61% to 73.9% from 2014-15 to 2020-21.
- Percentage of institutional deliveries improved from 87% to 94.8% from 2014-15 to 2020-21.
- Girls/women have a remarkable 43% presence in STEM fields, showcasing one of the highest rates globally in 2023.

Indian Army had 1,733 women officers.
Indian Navy had 580 women officers.
Armed forces medical services had 6,466 women officers (Army, Navy, Airforce).
By july 2023.

8. 'Viksit Bharat': Armed Forces' Gender Equality Milestone

The Indian Armed Forces have ushered in a historic era of gender inclusivity, extending permanent commission opportunities to women, referred to as 'Durga' and 'Shakti', across diverse roles. Women now serve on warships, assume specialised Naval Air Operations (NAO) roles and operate ship-borne helicopters in the Indian Navy. In a groundbreaking move, they are integrated into all combat roles of the Indian Air Force and have even attained the rank of Colonel in the Indian Army. This transformative decision, fostering a 'Viksit Bharat' or developed India, was officially proclaimed by Prime Minister Narendra Modi from the iconic Red Fort on the 72nd Independence Day.

- The Indian Army had 1,733 women officers (excluding medical) and 100 other ranks as of January 2023.
- Women officers (excluding medical) in the Indian Air Force were 1,654, with 155 airwomen by July 2023.
- The Indian Navy had 580 women officers (excluding medical) and 726 sailors by July 2023.
- Armed Forces medical services had 6,466 women officers (Army, Navy, Air Force) by July 2023.
- Republic Day 2024: Kartavya Path parade featured all-women contingents, bands and tableaux in a historic move for gender equality.

BANK
In 2023, SSY provided highest rate of interest at 8%.
SUKANYA SAMRIDDHI YOJANA

9. Guardians of Dreams: Sukanya Samriddhi Yojana

Sukanya Samriddhi Yojana (SSY), a beacon of financial empowerment in 'Viksit Bharat', is a radiant opportunity unveiled by the visionary Prime Minister on 22 January, 2015. Crafted by the Ministry of Finance, this small deposit marvel is a sanctuary for a girl child's dreams. Nestled in post offices and esteemed branches of commercial banks, the SSY account, adorned with the dreams of education and marriage, welcomes guardians with open arms. As the clock of time ticks, the account, curated with love, grows for 21 years, providing tax-exemption benefits and a nurturing cocoon fostering in a promising future for the daughters of 'Viksit Bharat'.

- The minimum investment is ₹250 per annum; The maximum investment is ₹1 50,000 per annum.
- In 2023, SSY provided the highest rate of interest at 8%.
- Principal, interest and maturity benefits in Sukanya Samriddhi Yojana are tax-exempted under Section 80C.
- At 18 years, up to 50% of the investment can be withdrawn prematurely, even if marriage is not imminent.
- Since inception, the scheme has seen 2.73 crore accounts opened with deposits totalling nearly ₹1.19 lakh crore.

Sambal
Beti bachao-
beti padhao
Nari adalat
Women
helplines
Samarthya
Shakti niwas
Shakti sadan
Hub for
empowerment
of women

10. 'Mission Shakti': A Pledge for Women's Progress

The government's vision for 'Viksit Bharat' is embodied in 'Mission Shakti', a pivotal initiative during the 15th Finance Commission period. This mission is dedicated to fortifying interventions for women's safety, security and empowerment, aligning with the commitment to 'women-led development'. By addressing women's issues across the life-cycle continuum, fostering citizen ownership and enhancing convergence among ministries and departments, 'Mission Shakti' envisions women as equal partners in nation-building. The sub-schemes, 'Sambal' and 'Samarthya', underscore the dual focus on ensuring the safety and security of women and empowering them to actively contribute to India's holistic development.

- Total outlay of ₹20,989 crore for 'Mission Shakti' in the 15th Finance Commission period, with a Central share of ₹15,761 crores.
- Budget allocation (2023-24) of ₹3,146.96 crores, with ₹562 crores for 'Sambal' and ₹2,581.96 crores for 'Samarthya'.
- 'Beti Bachao,Beti Padhao', Nari Adalat and Women Helplines are components under 'Sambal'.
- Sakhi Niwas, Shakti Sada and Hub for Empowerment of Women are components under 'Samarthya'.
- 'Mission Shakti' reflects India's commitment to fulfilling international obligations, including the United Nations' Sustainable Development Goals.

□

DIGITAL DAWN

Section-3

Digital Dawn

"India's digital public infrastructure offers scalable, secure and inclusive solutions for global challenges."

—Prime Minister Shri Narendra Modi
(G20 Digital Economy Ministers' Meet,
Bengaluru on 19.08.2023)

BY DECEMBER 2023, EGRAMSWARAJ-4 HAS EMPOWERED 2.78 LAKH PANCHAYATI RAJ INSTITUTIONS WITH ONLINE SERVICES AND DIGITAL LITERACY.
Government office
UMANG

11. Governance Evolves at Your Fingertips

Gone are the days of navigating endless paperwork and frustrating delays. India's digital revolution is reshaping governance, making it accessible, transparent and empowering for all. Here are five ways technology is transforming lives across the nation. This digital leap is not just a trend; it's a promise for a future where technology empowers, transparency reigns and good governance becomes the norm. Download, engage and be a part of this transformative journey of 'Viksit Bharat'. The power of change is just a click away in 'Amrit Kaal'.

- By December 2023, e-GramSwaraj-4 has empowered 2.78 lakh Panchayati Raj institutions with online services and digital literacy.
- Access 1,811+ government services, ranging from healthcare to education, in 23 Indian languages through the UMANG app with just a tap.
- As of December 2023, DigiLocker, the national document wallet on the cloud, has empowered 225.98+ million citizens.
- Join the MyGov community as 30.84+ crore people became MyGov *saathis* by December 2023, fostering increased public participation.
- Transforming Bharat dashboards allows citizens to track key government schemes and promote transparency in governance.

6.4 LAKH VILLAGES WITH HIGH SPEED BROADBAND NETWORKS BY 2025
COMMON SERVICE CENTER

12. BharatNet: Weaving a Digital India, Pixel by Pixel

Forget patchy connections and digital deserts, BharatNet, India's expansive fibre optic highway, overcomes connectivity challenges, bridging digital gaps. Each cable kilometre weaves a technological tapestry, establishing the world's largest rural broadband initiative with a 1.39 lakh crore budget. The ambitious goal is to connect 6.4 lakh villages with high-speed broadband networks by 2025. Global attention is drawn to its economic impact reflected in headlines like 'India's Fibre-Optic Revolution' (*The Financial Times*) and 'Connecting the Unconnected' (*The Wall Street Journal*). Envisioned for empowerment, BharatNet steers towards inclusivity, contributing to the vision of the 'Viksit Bharat'.

- Since 2018, 6.64 lakh kilometres of optical fibre were laid in the country by December 2023.
- 2.08 lakh *gram panchayats* are already empowered with services out of the total 2.64 lakh planned as of December 2023.
- BharatNet has already created 12 lakh jobs by December 2023 and is projected to generate ₹1 lakh crore by 2025, showcasing its economic impact.
- India's first ever undersea 2,312 km-long optical fibre project was completed in 2018, connecting Chennai with Andaman and Nicobar Islands.
- Kochi with Lakshadweep Islands submarine optical-fibre connection projects of 1989.19 kms were completed on 3 January 2024 within just 1,000 days.

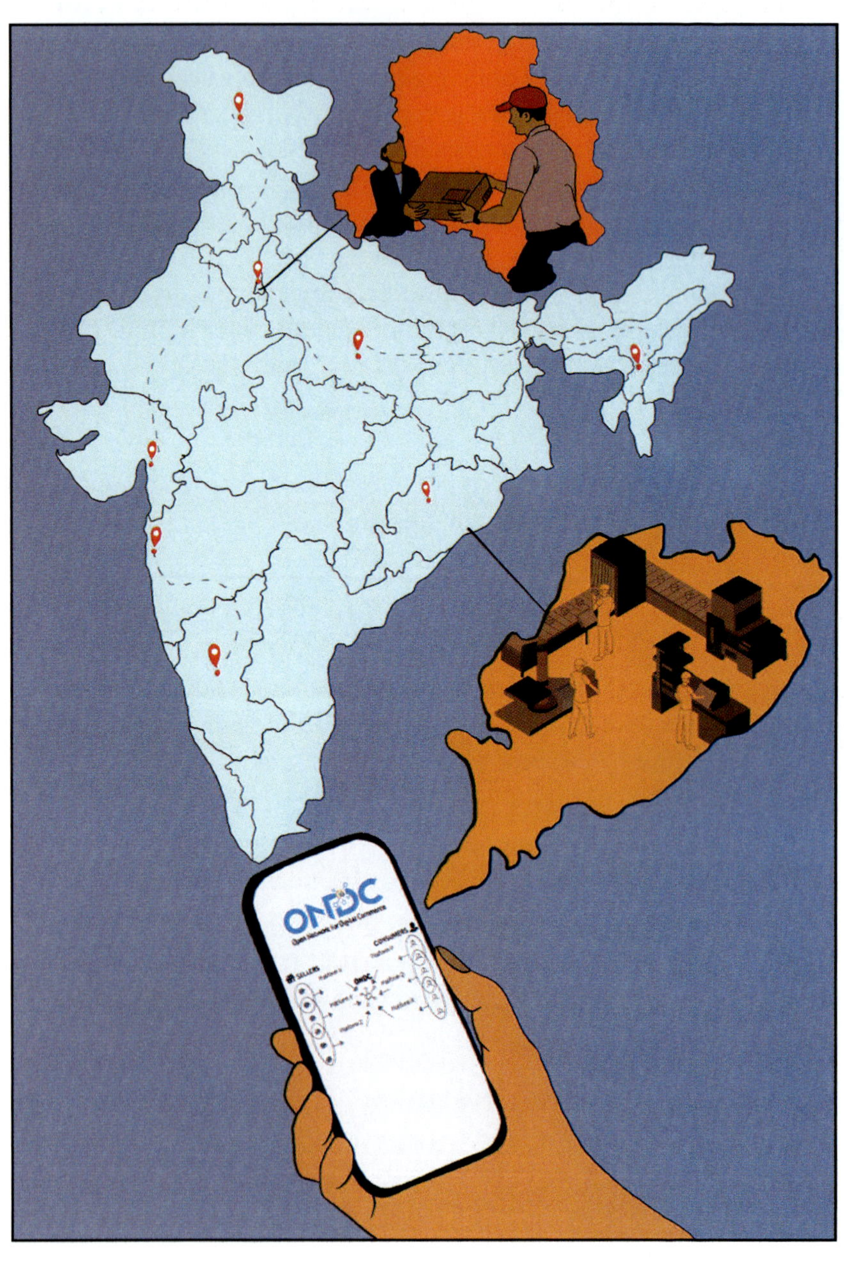
ONDC
CONSUMERS
SELLERS
ONDC

13. ONDC: Fuelling Open, Inclusive E-commerce in India

Ditch the gilded cages of closed platforms and platform fees. India's Open Network for Digital Commerce (ONDC) is revolutionising e-commerce like a tech-powered bazaar, empowering small businesses and bursting with potential. With the world's third-largest online shopper base, ONDC aims to elevate e-retail penetration from 4.3% in 2023, benefitting over 12 million sellers, particularly in small towns and villages. It's not just another marketplace; it's a paradigm shift. ONDC opens doors, fuels government revenue, empowers sellers to compete with large market players and becomes discoverable. It's not just a button; it's a portal to a vibrant, inclusive and truly Indian e-commerce future for 'Viksit Bharat'.

- ONDC was operationalised in over 500 cities and towns across the country as of December 2023.
- 2.37+ lakh sellers and service providers were onboard the ONDC portal as of December 2023.
- *₹1.5+ lakh crore potential by 2025*: Assam weavers reach urban fashionistas; Kerala spices dance in distant kitchens.
- *1.5 million new jobs by 2030*: AI whizzes build ONDC apps, delivery agents zoom through villages – a job creation powerhouse bridging the digital divide.
- Himalayan honey reaches city markets and Nagaland crafts connect globally. ONDC's open network welcomes rural sellers to the e-commerce party.

GeM
Government
e Marketplace
Efficient • Transparent • Inclusive
सत्यमेव जयते
TReDS
UDYAM
MSME
MICRO, SMALL & MEDIUM ENTERPRISES
Registration
3+ crore MSMEs
registered on udyam
As on december 2023

14. E-Procurement: Viksit Engine Hums

Forget opaque corridors and limited access. India's e-procurement portals are rewriting the script, boosting transparency, efficiency and opportunities for small and medium enterprises. These portals are not just numbers; they empower businesses, streamline processes and propel the country's economic engine. GeM ensures transparent, efficient and inclusive public procurement, TReDS provides capital access to credit-starved small businesses and the Udyam portal enables zero cost and quick registration for MSMEs. This is the future these portals are paving the way for, brick by digital brick for 'Viksit Bharat'.

- Since its 2016 launch, GeM has processed ₹6.3 lakh crore in transactions by October 2023.

  GeM has over 1.7+ lakh registered sellers, including 70,000+ MSMEs.

  Launched in 2014, TReDS addresses MSME liquidity challenges by allowing them to discount invoices.

- It has resulted in over ₹1.4 lakh crore worth of invoices discounted by October 2023, effectively lowering financing costs for MSMEs.

- Launched in 2020, Udyam portal had over 3 crore MSMEs by December 2023 and out of which 41 lakhs were owned by women.

PERSONAL DIGITAL DATA

15. People-centric DPDP: India's Digital Overhaul

The Digital Personal Data Protection Act, passed in August 2023, marks a new era – not just for data, but for our citizens. It empowers them, transforms anxieties into confidence and paints a future where technology is a tool, not a master. Unchecked processing poses privacy risks, a recognised fundamental right, highlighting the importance of this Act. It isn't just a legislation; it's a canvas, a reimagining of India's digital data landscape. From rural farmers accessing land records online to remote patients receiving care through DP DP-compliant platforms, empowered individuals are shaping a vibrant future for 'Viksit Bharat'.

- *Empowered consumers*: Securely access personal data, enabling informed choices and unlocking financial opportunities.
- It gives rights to an individual to access information of personal data, correction or erasure of data, grievance redressal, etc.
- The Act spurs a ₹5 lakh crore revenue gain by 2025 through increased consumer spending and tax collection.
- *One million new jobs*: Data security, compliance and ethical AI solutions create a thriving data protection ecosystem.
- Data fiduciary boosts e-commerce, benefiting small businesses in India.

□

ATMANIRBHAR ASCEND

Section-4

Atmanirbhar Ascend

"We must strive vigorously for 'Atmanirbhar Bharat'. It becomes the responsibility of every citizen, every government and every unit of society. 'Atmanirbhar Bharat' is not a government agenda or a government programme; this is a mass movement of society which we have to achieve in 'Amrit Kaal'.

—Prime Minister Shri Narendra Modi

(76th Independence Day, Red Fort,
New Delhi on 15.08.2022)

Tamil Nadu Defence Industrial Corridor
Investment of INR 3,847+ crore has been made in TNDIC
Uttar Pradesh Defence Industrial Corridor
Investment of INR 2,242 crore has been made in UPDIC
Arjun
AKASH
AKASH
AKASH
As of December 2023

16. Crafting Power: Defence Manufacturing Surge

In the era of 'Amrit Kaal', the tapestry of new India's defence strength is intricately woven with threads of innovation, crafting a robust shield of self-reliance. Over the last 9.5 years, the nation's defence budget surged from ₹2.03 lakh crores in 2014 to ₹5.94 lakh crores in 2023. Simultaneously, India's defence exports reached an all-time high, surging from ₹686 crores in FY 2013-14 to nearly ₹16,000 crores in FY 2022-23. This remarkable 23-fold increase stands as a beacon, channelling focused and structured efforts towards enhancing the country's defence production capabilities, including aerospace and naval industries, with the ambitious goal of achieving US$ 5 billion in exports by 2025.

- Uttar Pradesh Defence Industrial Corridor attracted ₹ 2,242+ crores, while Tamil Nadu Defence Industrial Corridor secured ₹ 3,847+ crores in investments by 2023.
- Aim is to manufacture 5,000 defence components by 2025, currently imported, thereby enhancing self-reliance.
- Record 75 per cent (approx. ₹ one lakh crores) of the defence capital procurement budget was earmarked for domestic industry in FY 2023-24, up from 68 per cent in 2022-23.
- Till April 2023, 606 licences were issued to 369 defence-sector companies, thus driving industrial growth.
- Defence India startup challenge and iDex innovation hub promote innovation for Armed Forces' challenges through startups.

Micron
TATA
DELL
hp
flex
BHAGWATI
TechnoStar
Genus
PLI apporoved 23 companies are ready for immediate function.
PLI scheme for the semiconductor industry in India has a budget of INR 76.5 billion.
As on November 2023

17. Tech Thrust: Bharat Semiconductor Soar

'Amrit Kaal' navigates the silicon realms, crafting a future where innovation thrives and technology empowers. Recognised as the new oil, semiconductors are at the forefront of a mission to slash 25% from India's current $8 billion import bill. The transition from questioning 'Why invest' to asserting 'Why not invest' in Bharat for semiconductors within just 15 months underscores the nation's resolute commitment. Overcoming past challenges, Bharat charts a course towards becoming a developed nation by 2047, positioning itself as the global hub where semiconductors metamorphose into superconductors propelling the economy forward.

- PLI scheme allocates ₹76.5 billion for semiconductor industry's growth in five years.
- Micron invested $2.75 billion with government support for India's largest semiconductor plant; SIMTech allocated ₹1,250 crores for a chip component facility as of January 2024.
- 27 PLI-approved companies, 23 operational by November 2023, drive the progress of the semiconductor sector.
- PLI companies to invest ₹3,000 crores, adding production value of ₹3.5 lakh crores, thus creating 2 lakh jobs.
- AMD establishes India's largest design centre at Bengaluru, focusing on semiconductor technology design and development with an investment of $400 million till 2028.

ECONOMY
2014
2023
unacademy
lenskart
PhonePe
DREAM11
#startupindia
paytm
OYO
zomato
100+ UNICORNS IN INDIA, MORE TO COME.
INDIA COMES 3rd IN THE GLOBAL ECOSYSTEM

18. Innovate, Elevate, Transform: Startup India

India's startup saga, orchestrated by visionary minds, harmonises innovation with robust governance, sculpting a resilient ecosystem poised for excellence. The inception of Startup India in 2016 marked a pivotal stride towards fostering a robust startup environment, aiming to generate extensive employment and sustainable economic growth. Today, it thrives as a catalyst, revolutionising industries and reshaping markets. Notably, the majority of startups are run by youngsters under 35 years of age and one out of 10 unicorns globally are proudly Indian as of December 2023. This multifaceted initiative spans policy formulation, bolstering incubation facilities, offering financial aid and advocating for market support – a foundational step in erecting the skyscraper of 'Viksit Bharat', where innovation flourishes, economies thrive and opportunities abound.

- Bharat rises to third largest startup ecosystem, growing from 450 in 2015 to 1,15,000 by 2023.
- Fifty regulatory reforms enhance business ease, capital access and reduce compliance, fostering startup growth as of 2023.
- Startup India Hub & Showcase connect stakeholders, enabling sector-specific discovery and promoting collaboration.
- ₹945 crores sanctioned under SISFS for 2021-22 to 2024-25; ₹10,000 crore corpus under FFS.
- Startups enjoy 80% and 50% patent/trademark filing rebates and self-certification benefits for three to five years post-incorporation.

Before
After
PLI

19. PLI Wave: India's Economic Resurgence

Bharat strides towards the top five global economies, eyeing a $5 trillion milestone, driven by transformative Product Linked Initiative (PLI) schemes. With a budget surpassing 1.97 lakh crores, these schemes amplify manufacturing prowess and boost exports. Incentivising investments in plant, machinery, R&D and technology transfer, they anticipate generating 60 lakh new jobs by 2026. Crucial for Make in India, PLI cements India's stature as a global manufacturing hub. Beyond economic growth, these schemes pave the way for a developed Bharat, marking the onset of 'Amrit Kaal' and propelling Bharat into the echelons of the world's top three economies.

- PLI scheme targets 14 key sectors, approving 733 applications with an expected investment of ₹3.65 lakh crores as of March 2023.
- In November 2023, 27 companies were approved under PLI for IT hardware with ₹3,000 crore investments.
- ₹62,500 crore investment by March 2023 yielded (Does it mean one lakh or?) lakh crore production, 3,25,000 jobs and ₹2.56 lakh crore exports by FY 2022-23.
- Telecom sector achieved 60% import substitution; Bharat neared self-reliance in Antennae, GPON CPE.
- Actual investment of ₹ 62,500 crores till March 2023 led to ₹6.75 lakhs crore sales, creating 3,25,000 jobs.

Vocal For Local And Making It Global
Ground Nut Oil
Walnut
Jaggery
Black Rice
Makhana
Amla
Millets
Toys

20. Local to Global: ODOP Revolution

The mantra of 'Vocal for Local and Making it Global', bestowed by Prime Minister Shri Narendra Modi, has evolved into a widespread movement, fostering indigenous products and uplifting small-scale enterprises and local artisans. The One District One Product-District as Export Hub (ODOP-DEH) initiative serves as a framework for value chain development and aligning support infrastructure, encompassing common services and product marketing. It specifically identifies perishable local products, from millets and fruits to pickles, poultry, handloom and handicrafts. This initiative not only revitalises the local product market but also empowers individuals associated with these sectors in the era of 'Amrit Kaal', making self-reliant districts.

- The aim is to turn each district into a manufacturing and export hub by identifying local products.
- The District Exports Promotion Committee constituted across 36 states and UTs has identified products across 765 districts.
- Indian toy industry witnessed a 52% decline in imports and a 239% rise in exports in FY 2022-23 in comparison to FY 2014-15.
- The Director General of Foreign Trade and Amazon have identified 75 districts for capacity building to handhold potential e-commerce exporters as per MOU in November 2023.
- A total of 26 districts were shortlisted for export of jute as of 2023.

□

AMRIT PEEDHI
KHELO INDIA
MUDRA YOJNA
ROZGAR MELA
SKILL INDIA MISSION
Anshul Gupta

Section-5

Youth Empowerment and Sports Development

"In new India, development is giving way to new opportunities for the youth and the youth are giving new wings to the development of the country."

—Prime Minister Shri Narendra Modi
(Foundation Stone of 508 Amrit Bharat Stations on 06.08.2023)

Skilling surge :
2.5 crore trained /certified by 2023, 35 lakh skilled worker entering annually
Rural reach :
PMKKs in 738 districts 80+lakhs rural residents (5 lakh pre-2014)
PMKVY
Digital skilling:
1 crore individuals accessed in 2023 (400%)increased since 2020
Entrepreneurial spark:
8 lakh + trained in entrepreneurship, created 5 lakh micro -enterprises annually.
1.24 + crore accessed candidates under PMKVY
Anshul Gupta

21. Skill India Mission: Empowering Employability

Launched in 2015, the Skill India Mission underscores India's commitment to enhancing its workforce's skills. Addressing the gap between talent and industry needs, the initiative, led by the Ministry of Skill Development and Entrepreneurship, focuses on providing market-relevant skills. With 2,750+ operational standard courses on NSDC, schemes like SANKALP, Pradhan Mantri Kaushal Vikas Yojana, Jan Shikshan Sansthan, and National Apprenticeship Promotion Scheme contribute to skill, re-skill and up-skill training, fostering entrepreneurship. This strategic approach aims to boost overall national competitiveness by aligning workforce capabilities with industry's requirements.

- Training increased from 30 lakh to 2.5 crores+ by 2023, boosting annual skilled workers to 35 lakh and employability by 20%.
- PMKKs in 738 districts empowered 80+ lakh rural residents, generating 15 lakh new rural jobs in 2023.
- In 2023, 1.24+ crore accessed candidates under the Pradhan Mantri Kaushal Vikas Yojana.
- Over 8 lakh people trained in entrepreneurship, resulting in 5 lakh micro-enterprises annually, surpassing pre-2014 levels.
- 60% of programmes co-designed with industry, led to a 35% increase in employment for skilled individuals and reduced skills mismatch by 20%.

ROZGAR
MELA
6.5 LAKH JOB
APPOINTMENT LETTER
IN 10 EDITIONS
Anshul
Gupta

22. Rozgar Melas: Catapulting Employment Opportunities

India's employment landscape is undergoing a significant transformation propelled by initiatives like the Rozgar Mela. Launched in 2022, these job fairs act as catalysts for job creation, connecting skilled individuals with diverse opportunities with 40-50 employers from 10-12 high-growing economic sectors. The Rozgar Mela, a half-day event, streamlines the interaction between employers and job seekers, expediting the employment process. Alongside, tools such as the e-Shram portal and Rozagar Yojana play vital roles, empowering the 'Amrit Peedhi' generation for the development of a skilled India.

- 6.5 lakh youth recruited in 10 editions, addressing employment needs effectively by October 2023.
- Recruits trained via the iGOT Karmayogi portal, offering 400+ e-learning courses for flexible learning.
- 1.92 crore vacancies created on the National Career Service portal by December 2023, enhancing employment prospects.
- Targeted Rozgar Melas in rural districts allocate 30% vacancies for the rural workforce, fostering inclusive growth.
- ₹10,043.02 crores disbursed to 60.48 lakh beneficiaries through Atmanirbhar Bharat Rozgar Yojana, promoting self-reliant employment

• 2841 ATHLETES IDENTIFIED
• 900+ KHELO INDIA CENTRES
KHELO INDIA
KHELO INDIA
KHELO INDIA
05
07
02
Ashul Gupta

23. Khelo India and TOPS: Shaping Global Sporting Dominance

India's sporting future isn't whispered in hopeful dreams; it roars with triumphant certainty, fuelled by the transformative Khelo India initiative. Launched in 2017, Khelo India isn't just nurturing grassroots talent; it's shaping Olympic champions and rewriting India's global sporting narrative. 25% surge in Olympics medals since 2017 and 100+ medals in Asian and Para-Asian Games 2023 are the results of the Khelo India initiative. There are 285 athletes under Target Olympic Podium Scheme, TOPS, focusing on world-class training and financial assistance as of 2023. It aims at modernising sports infrastructure at the grassroots while providing scientific training to young athletes, all with the help of technology to enhance the sports ecosystem for 'Viksit Bharat'.

- 2,841 athletes from 21 sports disciplines identified under Khelo India talent development as of December 2023.
- Over 1,000 academies (10x from 2017) empower rural talent, boosting sports like weightlifting and *kabaddi*.
- 900+ Khelo India centres covering 600+ districts and training 13,000+ athletes and 297 sports infrastructure projects sanctioned.
- 2,000+ athletes receive annual scholarships aiding champions and 23,000+ athletes and 237 academies supported as of December 2023.
- First ever Khelo India para games were organised in New Delhi in December 2023 with the participation of 1,400 players from 32 states.

MUDRA LOAN
44 CRORE OF MUDRA LOANS GIVEN
Anshul Gupta

24. Microfinance, Macro Impact: Mudra Yojana

Launched in April 2015, the transformative Mudra Yojana has ignited India's micro-enterprise sector, offering loans up to ₹10 lakhs to non-corporate, non-farm small/micro enterprises. Involving diverse financial entities, such as MFIs, NBFCs, Small Finance Banks and more, Mudra facilitates low-interest personal loans, proving instrumental in generating extensive grassroots employment. A game-changer for 'Viksit Bharat', Mudra has significantly contributed to job creation and economic growth since its inception.

- Over 44.46 crore loans sanctioned worth ₹ 27.5+ lakh crores since its inception by December 2023.
- 30.64 crores, i.e. 69% of the total beneficiaries are women entrepreneurs.
- 51% of loans belong to entrepreneurs of SC/ST and OBC categories out of the total sanctioned loans as of 2023.
- Loans categorised as Shishu (up to ₹50,000), Kishore (above ₹50,000 to ₹5 lakh) and Tarun (above ₹5 lakh to ₹10 lakh).
- Entrepreneurs receive skill training through PMMY, leading to lakhs of new jobs annually and fostering sustainable growth.

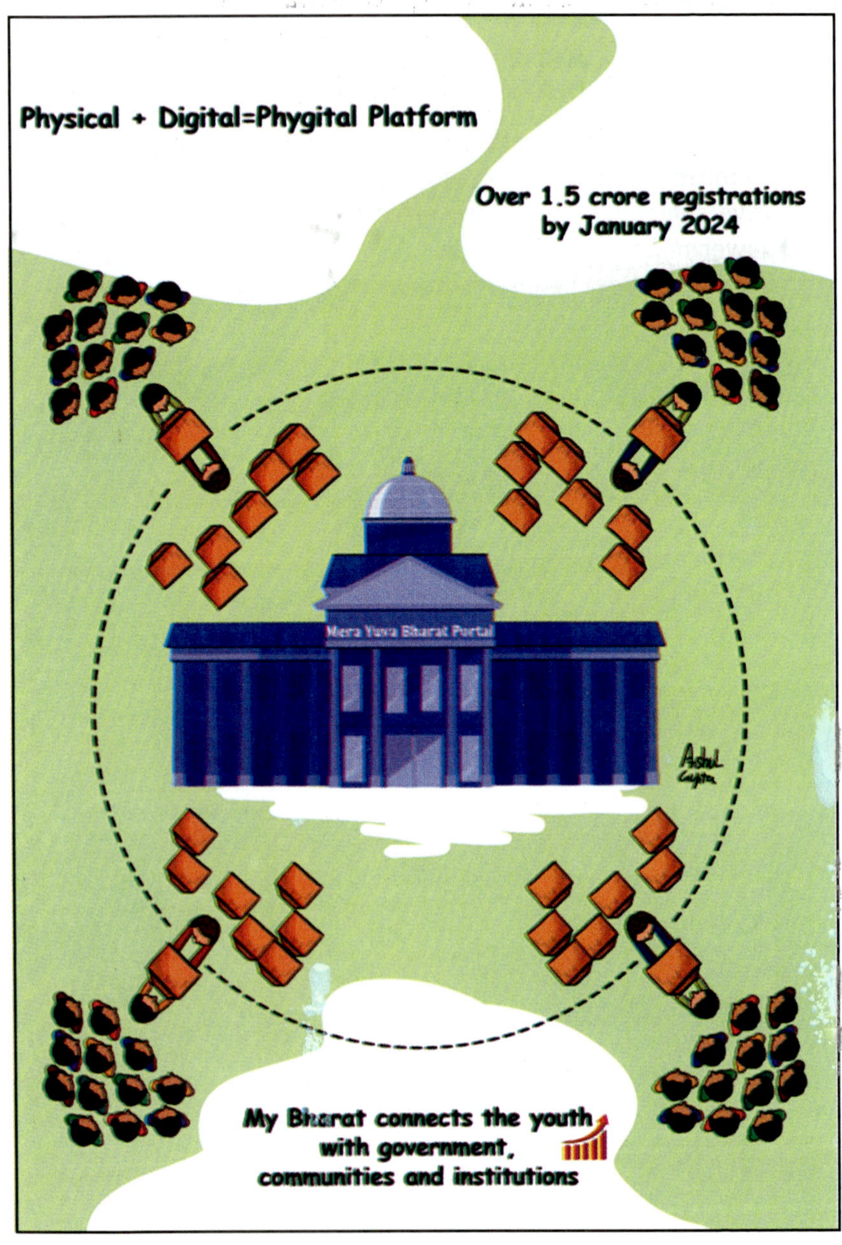
Physical + Digital=Phygital Platform
Over 1.5 crore registrations by January 2024
Mera Yuva Bharat Portal
My Bharat connects the youth with government, communities and institutions

25. Connecting Dreams: Mera Yuva Bharat's Vision

The question in every youngster's mind, 'How can I find opportunities for national development through self-development' has an answer. 'Mera Yuva Bharat' is a transformative, technology-driven platform launched on 31 October, 2023, envisioning youth as a potent force for positive societal change. The initiative aims to unify youth empowerment and engagement opportunities on a single platform. To provide equitable opportunities, 'Mera Yuva Bharat' seeks to enable the youth to realise their aspirations and contribute to the creation of a developed Bharat ('Viksit Bharat'). The platform facilitates seamless connections for the youth in social, governmental and economic sectors by opening the doors of opportunities for self and national development.

- This physical + digital = phygital platform aims to cater to all youth-related opportunities in a single window.
- Over 1.5+ crore youngsters have registered on the portal and joined the journey to 'Viksit Bharat'.
- 'My Bharat' enables the youth to connect with government institutions, non-profit organisations and business entities.
- Improving the alignment between youth aspirations and community needs while enhancing efficiency through converging existing programmes.
- It also provides experiential learning opportunities like internships, fellowships, etc.

□

ECONOMIC EVOLUTION

ENVISIONING TO BE THE THIRD LARGEST ECONOMY OF THE WORLD

Section-6

Economic Evolution

"Bharat will become the world's third largest economy and by 2047, it will become a developed country, India's economic growth is linked to the progress of the entire world."

—Prime Minister Narendra Modi
(IAADB Inauguration, Red Fort on 09.12.2023)

$2 TRILLION IN 2014.
$4 TRILLION IN 2023.
SET AT $5 TRILLION IN 2025.
CORPORATE DEBT SHRANK BY 12% OF GDP FROM 2015 TO 2023.
FDI SOARED 57 TIMES, LEAPING FROM $45.15 BILLION IN 2014 TO $71 BILLION IN 2022-23
18 COUNTRIES EMBRACED THE INDIAN NATIONAL RUPEE FOR TRADE OVER THE U.S. DOLLAR
INDIA'S PER CAPITA INCOME DOUBLED TO ₹1.97 LAKHS SINCE 2014.
AS OF DECEMBER 2023.

26. 'Amrit Kaal': India's Economic Odyssey

India's economic journey is remarkable: it took nearly six decades to reach a $1 trillion economy, just over a decade to hit $2 trillion in 2014 and now, in less than a decade, it has surged to a $4 trillion economy. The ambitious target is set at $5 trillion by 2025, propelling Bharat from the tenth to the fifth largest economy globally in less than 10 years. This rapid ascent, from being labelled part of the 'fragile five' by Morgan Stanley in 2013 to being hailed as the 'fastest growing economy' in 2023 by the same institution, reflects a committed and visionary governance approach during the transformative decade defining the 'Amrit Kaal'.

- Corporate debt shrank by 12% of GDP from 2015 to 2023.
- FDI soared 57 times, leaping from $45.15 billion in 2014 to $71 billion in 2022-23.
- 18 countries embraced the Indian national rupee for trade over the US dollar.
- Despite global challenges, India's GDP hit over 7 in Q2 FY23, showcasing economic strength.
- In 2023, India's per capita income doubled to ₹1.97 lakhs since 2014.

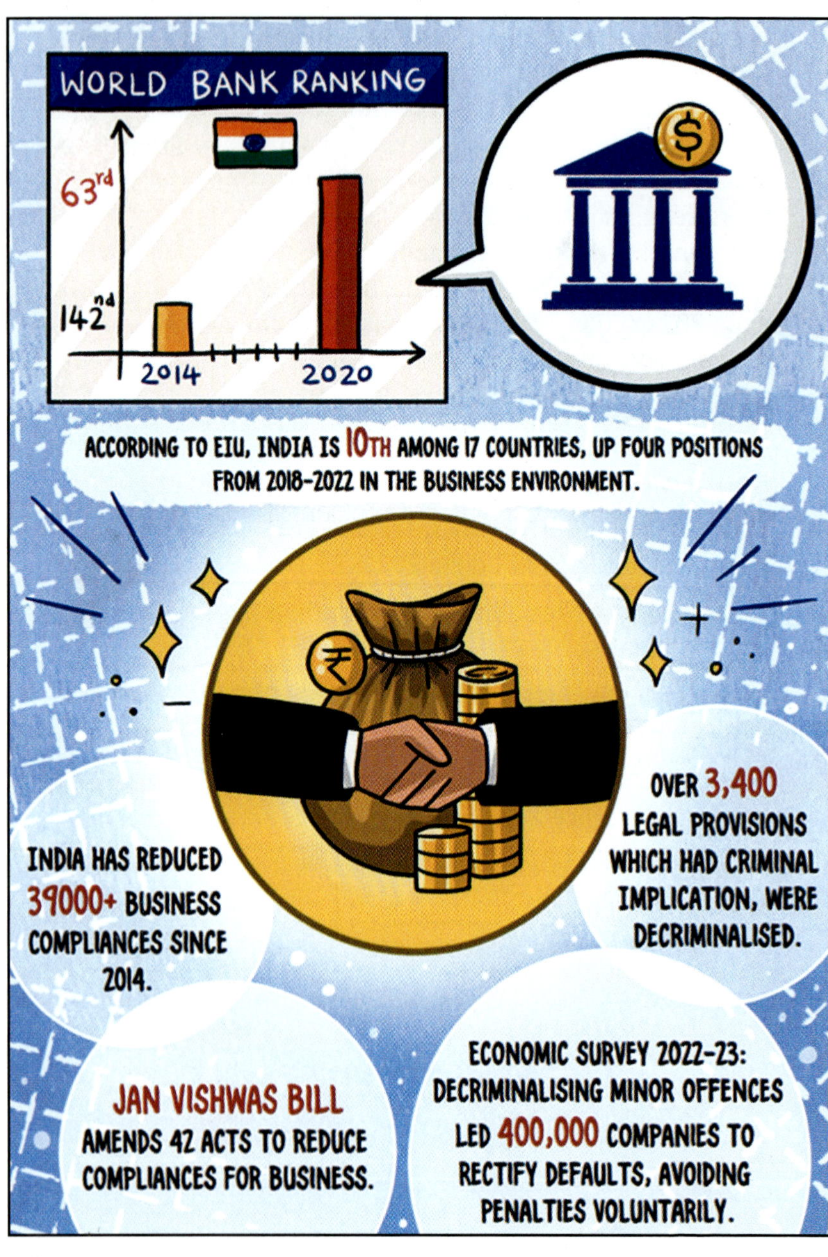
WORLD BANK RANKING
63rd
142nd
2014
2020
ACCORDING TO EIU, INDIA IS 10TH AMONG 17 COUNTRIES, UP FOUR POSITIONS FROM 2018-2022 IN THE BUSINESS ENVIRONMENT.
INDIA HAS REDUCED 39000+ BUSINESS COMPLIANCES SINCE 2014.
OVER 3,400 LEGAL PROVISIONS WHICH HAD CRIMINAL IMPLICATION, WERE DECRIMINALISED.
JAN VISHWAS BILL
AMENDS 42 ACTS TO REDUCE COMPLIANCES FOR BUSINESS.
ECONOMIC SURVEY 2022-23: DECRIMINALISING MINOR OFFENCES LED 400,000 COMPANIES TO RECTIFY DEFAULTS, AVOIDING PENALTIES VOLUNTARILY.

27. Ease of Doing Business: India's Transformation Tale

Pre-2014, 'ease of doing business' was unfamiliar in India. Soaring from 142nd in 2014 to 63rd in the 2020 World Bank ranking resulted from visionary governance. Bharat markedly enhanced its business climate through GST, digital reforms and streamlined regulations. The government's dedication to cutting bureaucratic red tape created a business-friendly landscape, drawing both domestic and global investments. Since 2014, this approach has laid the foundation for 'Viksit Bharat' – a developed Bharat in 2014.

- Bharat has reduced 39,000+ business compliances since 2014.
- According to EIU, Bharat is 10th among 17 countries, up four positions from 2018-22 in the business environment.
- Over 3,400 legal provisions, which had criminal implications, were decriminalised.
- *Economic survey 2022-23*: Decriminalising minor offences led 400,000 companies to rectify defaults, avoiding penalties voluntarily.
- Jan Vishwas Act amends 42 Acts to reduce compliances for businesses.

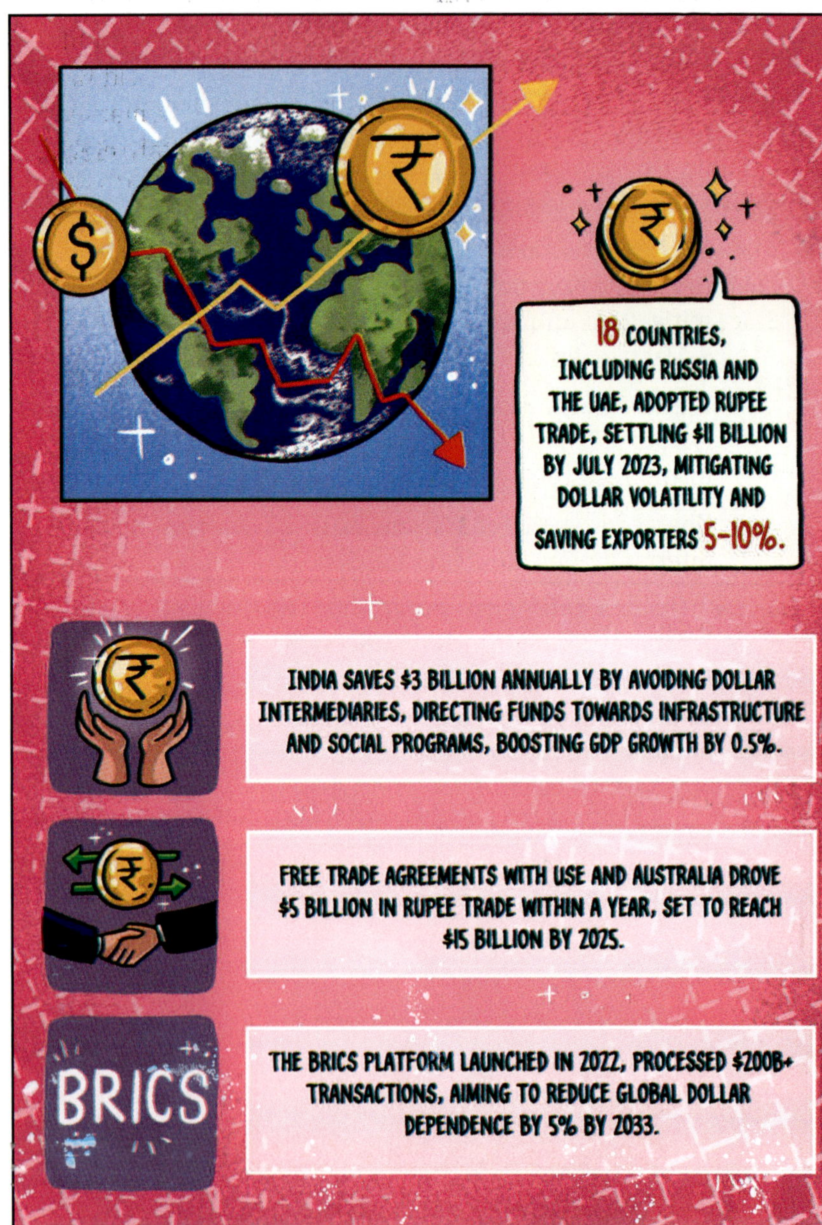
18 COUNTRIES, INCLUDING RUSSIA AND THE UAE, ADOPTED RUPEE TRADE, SETTLING $11 BILLION BY JULY 2023, MITIGATING DOLLAR VOLATILITY AND SAVING EXPORTERS 5-10%.
INDIA SAVES $3 BILLION ANNUALLY BY AVOIDING DOLLAR INTERMEDIARIES, DIRECTING FUNDS TOWARDS INFRASTRUCTURE AND SOCIAL PROGRAMS, BOOSTING GDP GROWTH BY 0.5%.
FREE TRADE AGREEMENTS WITH USE AND AUSTRALIA DROVE $5 BILLION IN RUPEE TRADE WITHIN A YEAR, SET TO REACH $15 BILLION BY 2025.
BRICS
THE BRICS PLATFORM LAUNCHED IN 2022, PROCESSED $200B+ TRANSACTIONS, AIMING TO REDUCE GLOBAL DOLLAR DEPENDENCE BY 5% BY 2033.

28. India's Rupee Revolution: Trade Freedom Blooms!

For decades, the global trade stage bowed to the greenback. But new India, a rising titan, is rewriting the script with its rupee trade revolution – a move not just about invoices, but about economic independence and dedollarisation's rising crescendo. Here's why India's rupee waltz is shaking the world in 'Amrit Kaal' aimed at 'Viksit Bharat'.

- 18 countries, including Russia and the UAE, adopted India's rupee trade, settling $11 billion by July 2023, mitigating dollar volatility and saving exporters 5-10%.
- Rupee settlements drive a projected $70 billion export surge by 2025, elevating revenue by 15% and fortifying India's global trade position.
- Bharat saves $3 billion annually by avoiding dollar intermediaries, directing funds toward infrastructure and social programmes and boosting GDP growth by 0.5%.
- Free trade agreements with UAE and Australia drove $5 billion in rupee trade within a year, set to reach $15 billion by 2025.
- The BRICS platform, launched in 2022, processed $200B+ transactions, aiming to reduce global dollar dependence by 5% by 2033.

GST REMOVES THE CASCADING EFFECT ON THE SALES OF GOODS AND SERVICES WHICH HAS IMPACTED THE COSTS OF GOODS, ELIMINATING THE TAX ON TAX, THE COST OF GOODS DECREASES.
GST MINIMISES TRANSPORTATION CYCLE TIMES, IMPROVES SUPPLY CHAIN AND TURNAROUND TIME, & LEADS TO WAREHOUSE CONSOLIDATION.
VAT
GST
GOODS & SERVICES TAX
COST REDUCTION!
Tax Simplification
CREDIT CARD
made in India

32. Revolutionising Tax: India's GST Triumph

India's intricate indirect tax structure found resolution with the introduction of the Goods and Services Tax (GST) in 2017, embodying the vision of One Nation One Tax. This landmark reform not only streamlined the nation's indirect tax system but also harmonised laws and rates across Central and state jurisdictions, fostering a unified market. By replacing erstwhile taxes like VAT and excise duty, GST significantly bolstered the ease of doing business, curbing tax evasion and corruption. Reverberating with positive impacts, this decision stands as a cornerstone in the economic development of new Bharat during the transformative era of 'Amrit Kaal'.

- GST boosts 'Make in India', enhancing competitiveness in national and global markets.
- GST removes tax on tax, reducing the cost of goods and eliminating the cascading effect.
- GST minimises transportation cycle times, improving supply chains, turnaround times and warehouse consolidation.
- Charging at all supply-chain levels, GST significantly cuts product prices, benefiting consumers.
- The average monthly gross GST collection of ₹1.66 lakh crore in the first nine-month period of 2023, indicates economic growth.

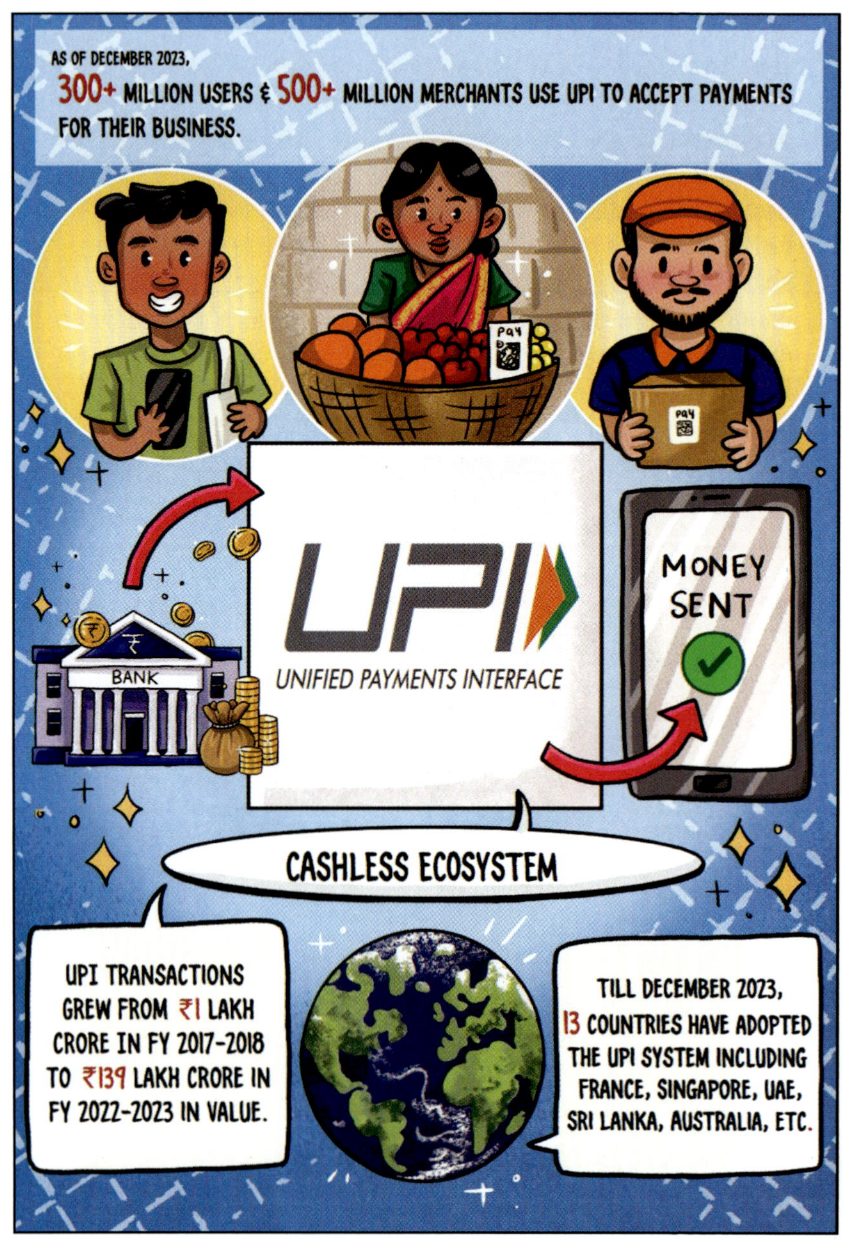
AS OF DECEMBER 2023,
300+ MILLION USERS & 500+ MILLION MERCHANTS USE UPI TO ACCEPT PAYMENTS FOR THEIR BUSINESS.
Pay
Pay
BANK
UPI
UNIFIED PAYMENTS INTERFACE
MONEY SENT
CASHLESS ECOSYSTEM
UPI TRANSACTIONS GREW FROM ₹1 LAKH CRORE IN FY 2017-2018 TO ₹139 LAKH CRORE IN FY 2022-2023 IN VALUE.
TILL DECEMBER 2023, 13 COUNTRIES HAVE ADOPTED THE UPI SYSTEM INCLUDING FRANCE, SINGAPORE, UAE, SRI LANKA, AUSTRALIA, ETC.

33. Digital Empowerment: UPI's Trail-blazing Journey

From a 5-star hotel in Lutyens Delhi to a tea-stall in Uttarakhand's Mana village, Bharat signifies a rapid shift toward a cashless ecosystem. In the past decade, the inconceivable idea of QR code-enabled money transfers for purchases, from vegetables to refrigerators, has become a reality through UPI. This cutting-edge platform breaks traditional banking barriers, allowing seamless transactions via smartphones. As per data in 2022, Bharat had a 46% share in digital transactions globally. The Prime Minister of the Netherlands was amazed to experience the seamless experience of UPI from a street vendor, during his visit to Bharat in 2023. UPI, a financial trailblazer, facilitates instant and secure fund transfers, catalysing financial inclusivity and ushering in an era of cashless transactions and economic empowerment during 'Amrit Kaal'.

- NPCI launched UPI in 2016, revolutionising digital payments in India.
- UPI serves 300+ million users and 500+ million merchants in seamless business transactions.
- UPI hit a record ₹18.23 lakh crores in December 2023, up from ₹11.9 lakh crores in 2022.
- UPI transactions grew from ₹1 lakh crores in FY 2017-18 to ₹139 lakh crores in FY 2022-23 in value.
- Adopted by 13 countries, UPI's global reach includes France, Singapore, UAE, Sri Lanka and Australia.

THEN..
₹.1 SENT
15 paisa Recieved
NOW...
₹.1 SENT
₹.1 Recieved
DBT HAS SAVED GOVERNMENT REVENUE OF OVER USD 27 BILLION TILL DECEMBER 2022 BY ELIMINATING CORRUPTION AND LEAKAGES IN SUBSIDY TRANSFERS.
भारत सरकार
Government of India
आधार - सामान्य माणसाचा अधिकार
IT HAS INCREASED TRANSPARENCY AND ACCOUNTABILITY IN THE GOVERNANCE, ENABLING EFFECTIVE GOVERNANCE FOR 'VIKSIT BHARAT'.
AADHAR ENABLED DBT TRANSFER ENABLED ELIMINATION OF 41.1 MILLION FAKE LPG CONNECTIONS AND 42 MILLION DUPLICATE RATION CARDS.

34. DBT: Lives Transformed, Transparency Ensured

The bygone era, where a mere 15 paise reached the poor out of every ₹ one sent from Delhi, has given way to the transformative approach of Direct Benefit Transfer (DBT). This government initiative digitally channels subsidies and financial aid, ensuring precision in reaching the intended recipients. The innovative DBT model has injected over $86 billion directly into the lives of millions, catalysing socio-economic progress and enhancing transparency in welfare ecosystems. By integrating technology and governance, DBT realises the vision of 'Antyodaya', delivering every single rupee directly to the beneficiary's bank account in a single click, eradicating intermediaries and ensuring efficient fund distribution.

- *FY24 DBT transfers*: October 2023 – 3.2 trillion; forecasted FY24 end – 7 trillion.
- Aadhaar-enabled DBT eradicated 41.1 million fake LPG connections and 42 million duplicate ration cards.
- ₹2,73,093 crores saved through DBT until March 2022, curbing corruption and leakages in the subsidy.
- DBT delivers 10,000+ government services, including major schemes like Vishwakarma Yojana and MGNREGS.
- DBT enhances governance transparency, ensuring accountability and effective governance for 'Viksit Bharat'.

G20 SUMMIT
KASHMIR VALLEY
INDIA
POST-ABROGATION
5th August, 2019
POWER OF CENTRAL AGENCIES INCREASED RESULTING IN MAJOR DECLINE IN TERROR ACTS, AND ESTABLISHED PEACE & PROSPERITY BY ATTRACTING INVESTMENTS IN KASHMIR VALLEY.
PRE-ABROGATION
UNLIKE EARLIER, THE POWER OF INDIAN PARLIAMENT IS NOT JUST LIMITED TO DEFENCE, EXTERNAL AFFAIRS AND COMMUNICATION IN KASHMIR - INTEGRATING THE NATION DEMOCRATICALLY.
LAL CHOWK, SRINAGAR

35. Kashmir's Rebirth: Article 370 Revoked

The Indian tricolour fluttering over Lal Chowk in Srinagar and the prospect of hosting the G20 summit in the Kashmir Valley were once deemed unattainable dreams. A decade ago, Kashmir, which was in the news for stone pelting and terrorist attacks, is now past 2023 and in the news to receive investment proposals worth ₹88,915 crore. However, on the historic day of 5 August, 2019, the Indian Parliament orchestrated a momentous shift by passing the abrogation of Article 370 and 35A in Kashmir, redefining the constitutional landscape. This decisive action, such as the 'zero terror plan', paved the way for inclusive governance, regional equilibrium and collective progress, fostering unity and cohesiveness in Kashmir. It marked a paradigm shift towards a more harmonious future, embodying the true spirit of 'Ek Bharat, Shreshtha Bharat' after seven decades of Independence.

- Expanded powers of the Indian Parliament in Kashmir for defence, external affairs and communication, fostering democratic integration.
- In 2022-23, Kashmir's GDP doubled to ₹2.25 lakh crores from one lakh crore after the abrogation of Article 370 in 2019.
- Terrorist activities reduced from 7,217 in 2004-14 to 2,197 in 2014-23 and a reduction of 50% in martyrs from security forces.
- Organised stone pelting reduced from 2,654 incidents, 112 civilian deaths and 6,000+ civilian injuries in 2010 to zero in 2023.
- Historic December 2020 district development council elections in J&K marked by a 51.42% voter turnout.

□

ROOTS RENNAISSANCE
Anshul Gupta

Section-8

Roots Renaissance

"No country can move forward without valuing its heritage. Bharat is not only a nation but an idea and a culture."

—Prime Minister Shri Narendra Modi
(All India Institute of Ayurveda, 18.10.2018)

Shaitan Island
Yogender island
Khetrapal Island
Hoshiar Island
Somnath Island
Sekhon Island
Tarapore Island
Dhan Singh Island
कर्तव्य पथ
Kartavya Path

36. Colonial Erasure: Bharat's Unveiling in 'Amrit Kaal'

In 1947, Bharat gained Independence, but the true liberation unfolded after 75 years, meticulously erasing colonial imprints. The historic moment at the G20 summit, where Prime Minister Narendra Modi stood before the Bharat plaque, encapsulates the essence. Azadi ka Amrit Mahotsav dismantled colonial vestiges – from city names, roads, statues and educational curriculum to logos and laws. Amidst the cultural renaissance of 'Amrit Kaal', Bharat strides forward, fuelled by pride in our rich heritage, valiant freedom fighters and profound traditions. The journey leads to a developed Bharat, resonating with the spirit of progress.

- Andaman and Nicobar's 21 islands have been renamed after Paramveer Chakra awardees and Ross Island was renamed Subhash Chandra Bose Island in 2018.
- The Indian Navy shifted the ensign to 'Sham No Varunah' from St. George Cross, inspired by Chhatrapati Shivaji Maharaj.
- The statue of Subhash Chandra Bose at the India Gate canopy in New Delhi replaces that of King George V.
- Rediscovering and publishing British-banned literary works (1905-1942) from '*Bang Bhang*' to '*Quit India*'.
- New Delhi's Rajpath is now Kartavya Path, emphasising duties in a democracy.

The new complex has 888 seats in the Lok Sabha Chamber and 384 seats in the Rajya Sabha Chamber
SHILIP DEERGHA GALLERY

37. Lok Kalyan Gateways: The New Parliament's Grandeur

Bharat, revered as the mother of democracy and the world's largest democratic nation, ardently embraces positive transformation in its relentless pursuit of progress. As we forge ahead, envisioning a developed future, the necessity to update policies and laws from the British-era parliamentary framework becomes evident. The new Parliament building stands as a testament to Bharat's rich cultural heritage, seamlessly blending it with cutting-edge technology and modern infrastructure. Encompassing 65,000 square metres, the structure features the 'Ashok Stambh' with roaring lions on the top, unique 'Bharatiya Ghatika' at its core, flanked by six gates – '*makar*', '*gaja*', '*shardul*', '*ashwa*', '*hamsa*', and '*garuda*'. Together, these gates, symbolic of *lok kalyan*, usher in prosperity in 'Amrit Kaal'.

- Sengol's installation with Vedic chants symbolises a historic power transfer, marking a significant step towards self-governance.
- Shilp Deergha gallery, themed around eight concepts, features 255 crafts from 400 artisans across Bharat.
- The Lok Sabha and Rajya Sabha now accommodate 888 and 384 seats respectively, with a joint session capacity of 1,272 seats for fully digitised legislation.
- The platinum-rated green building saves 30% electricity compared to its predecessor.
- Materials, including a carpet woven by 900 artisans from UP over 10 lakh hours, are sourced from various districts nationwide.

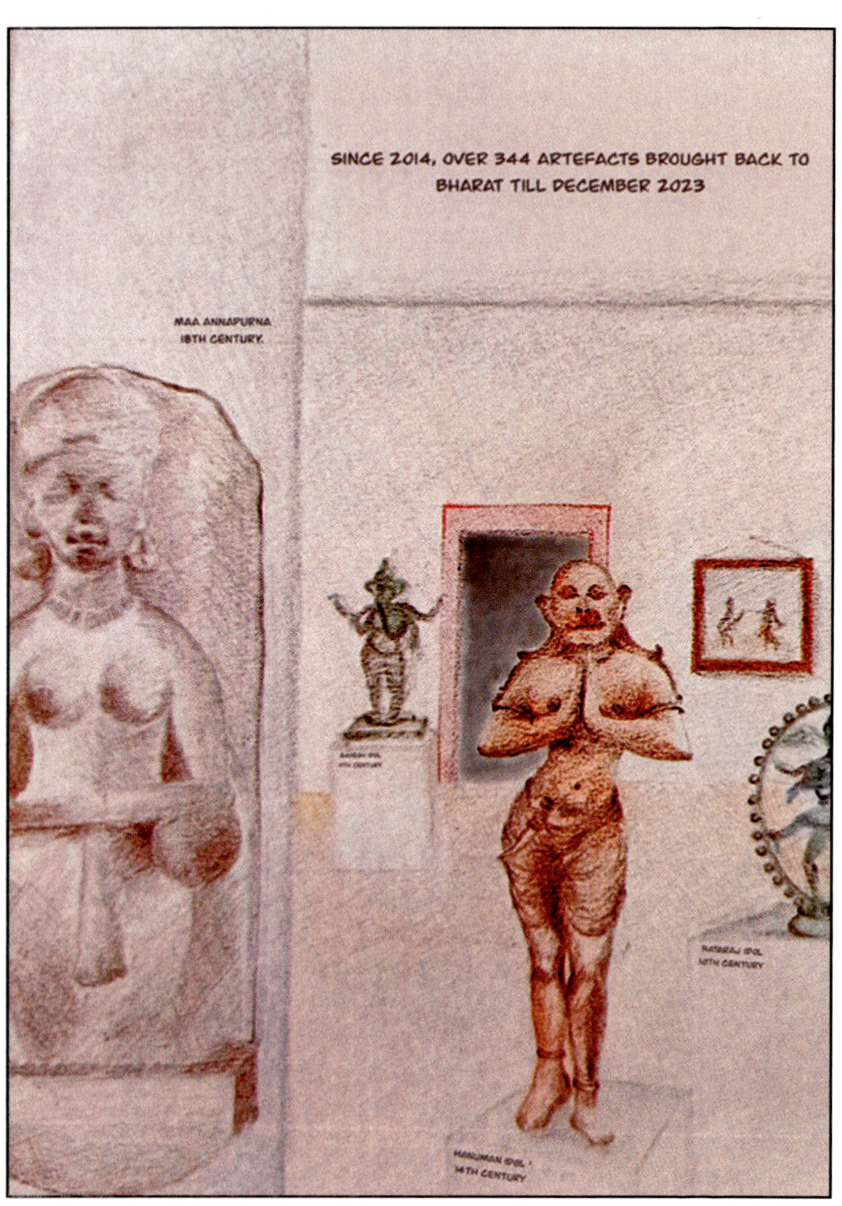
SINCE 2014, OVER 344 ARTEFACTS BROUGHT BACK TO BHARAT TILL DECEMBER 2023
MAA ANNAPURNA
18TH CENTURY.
NATARAJ IDOL
HANUMAN IDOL
14TH CENTURY

38. Heritage Reclaimed: India's Global Artifacts Retrieval

Bharat has been a land of art and sculptures since the ancient era. Post-2014, Prime Minister Narendra Modi spearheaded a renewed focus on the retrieval and preservation of ancient Indian artifacts, neglected for decades after Independence. Leveraging enhanced global relations, Bharat successfully reclaimed stolen cultural treasures, emphasising the importance of safeguarding its rich heritage. This proactive initiative not only symbolises a commitment to cultural preservation but also underscores India's diplomatic prowess in securing the return of these significant historical artifacts in 'Amrit Kaal'.

- From 2014-2023, over 344 artifacts were brought back to Bharat.
- In November 2021, a stolen 18th-century Maa Annapurna idol was returned to Varanasi, after a century-long absence, from Canada.
- An ancient Lord Hanuman idol from the late Chola period was recovered from Australia and returned to Bharat in 2023.
- Scotland returned a 14th-century ceremonial Indo-Persian sword and an 11th-century-stone door jamb seized from a Kanpur temple.
- The United States agreed to repatriate more than 105 stolen artifacts in 2023.

SHRI RAM MANDIR
AYODHYA
70 ACRES TEMPLE COMPLEX.
FULFILLED AFTER 500 YEARS

39. Cultural Resurgence: Temples of Bharat Reawaken

Centuries-old temples embody the spiritual core of the Bharatiya civilisation, resilient against ruthless attacks and foreign rule – a testament to enduring values. In the 'Amrit Kaal' era, seven decades post-Independence, restoring the Bharatiya civilisation's lost glory became imperative. The monumental Shri Ram Janmabhoomi temple, sprawling across 70 acres in Ayodhya, is became a reality on 22 January, 2024 – a historic day, realising a generational dream with its state-of-the-art construction. This revival echoes Bharat's principles of '*Sarve bhavantu sukhinah*' resonating globally, drawing tourism, boosting local economies and safeguarding cultural ethos – an essential stride in the development of 'Viksit Bharat'.

- Post the 2013 tragedy, Kedarnath Dham, including Shri Adi Shankaracharya's *samadhi*, was reconstructed and inaugurated in 2021, enhancing livelihood and pilgrim facilities.
- Varanasi's 'Kashi Vishwanath Corridor', inaugurated in 2021, revived 40 ancient temples over 5 lakh square feet, drawing 13 crore visitors in two years.
- Pavagadh Kalika temple unfurled its '*dhwaja*' after 500 years in a grand revamp in 2022.
- Ujjain's Mahakal Lok Corridor, unveiled in 2022, showcases cultural murals and idols across 900 metres, with 108 ornamental pillars.
- Post the 2019 abrogation of Article 370, temples are being restored and reopened across Kashmir, including Raghunath temple in 2020 and Sheetalnath temple in 2021, after 31 years.

"VOCAL FOR LOCAL"
Bhagavad Gita

40. Crafting Relations: Handloom Diplomacy of Bharat

Handloom and handicrafts embody Bharat's rich tradition, with approximately 31.44 lakh households engaged in the sector, as per the All India Handloom Census. In the past decade, the nation transitioned from gifting Taj Mahal models to presenting *Shrimad Bhagwad Gita* to global leaders. Prime Minister Shri Narendra Modi, advocating 'Vocal for Local', has become the foremost ambassador by gifting local artisan-crafted products. This not only showcases their skills but also empowers them, serving as a potent marketing tool for Indian handloom and handicrafts worldwide – contributing significantly to the vision of a developed Bharat.

- G7 leaders in 2022 were given black pottery (Nizamabad), a *gulabi meenakari* brooch (Varanasi) and a painted tea set (Bulandshahar).
- G20 leaders in 2023 were given a Pashmina stole (Kashmir), Muga silk stole (Assam), Kanjivaram stole (Tamil Nadu) and more in papier-mâché box and Kadam wood box.
- In 2023, US President Biden and First Lady were gifted lab-grown 7.5-carat green diamond, a carved sandalwood box.
- In 2023, the French President was given a sandalwood Sitar and Pochampally Ikkat for the First Lady.
- In 2022, European nation leaders were given Dhokara boat (Chhattisgarh), Koftgiri art piece (Rajasthan), Kutchi embroidery (Gujarat), etc.

□

REFORMING RAILWAYS
MODIFICATION
Anshul Gupta

Section-9

Reforming Railways

"Where the poor and middle class go, I will make those railway stations better than airports. We are working to make the rail journey accessible as well as pleasant. The effort is to provide the best possible experience from train to station."

—Prime Minister Shri Narendra Modi

(Jodhpur, Rajasthan on 05.10.2023)

AYODHYA JN
अयोध्या जं.
AMRIT BHARAT STATION
LOUNGE
WASHROOM
LOUNGE (A1 & A2)
WASHROOM
ONE STATION - ONE PRODUCT
ONE STATION
ONE PRODUCT
Ashul Gupta

41. Railway Station Renaissance: Amrit Bharat Stations

In pursuit of delivering world-class public amenities to its citizens, the Amrit Bharat station scheme, inaugurated in August 2023, is successfully modernising or upgrading a total of 1,309 railway stations. Remarkably, this figure equals the collective number of railway stations in South Africa (585), Russia (353) and Canada (410). The scheme is strategically designed to elevate the overall travel experience, fostering seamless integration between cities and their surrounding areas, while promoting multimodal transport facilities. Serving as a testament to the swift pace and expansive scale of development in 'Amrit Kaal', this initiative exemplifies the commitment of new Bharat to elevate public infrastructure standards.

- It will improve passenger amenities, like elevators and escalators, information displays, waiting halls, Wi-Fi, access points, circulating areas, etc.
- 'One Station, One Product' will boost local business and handicrafts.
- It will also create acres of urban spaces that will be nominated for business centres, meeting halls, executive lounges, etc.
- The station's theme would be such that it resembles the local culture and tradition of the city.
- Work began on 625+ stations and others were in various stages of planning within just six months of the scheme's announcement.

PRE 2014
Railway electrification is 32.7 %
POST 2024
Railway electrification is 100%
Ashok Gupta

42. Wired for Progress: India's Railway Electrification Feat

The transformation from 32.7% (21,413 kms) of broad-gauge railway electrification in 2014 to a remarkable 100% (65,350 kms) in 2023, marking a staggering 173% surge in just nine years, underscores Bharat's unwavering dedication to economical and environment-friendly railway operations. This achievement is equivalent to electrifying the entire railway networks of countries, such as Australia, Germany and Argentina within the same timeframe. A monumental leap in 'Amrit Kaal', it positions Indian Railways on the trajectory to achieve net-zero carbon emissions by 2030, eliminating 7.5 million tonnes of CO_2 annually. Beyond cost reduction, this stride fosters 'Atmanirbhar Bharat' by diminishing reliance on foreign countries for crude oil.

- Railway electrification of 1.7 RKM/day in 2013 to 18 RKM/day in 2023, indicates an electrifying pace in implementation.
- Electrification of all 411 maintenance pits aims to save around 2 lakh litres of fuel per day.
- Maintenance of diesel locomotives costs 32.84 thousand GTKM and the electric locomotive costs only 16.45 per thousand GTKM.
- The diesel consumption has also reduced by 50.29% and fuel expense shrank by 38% in 2020-21 as compared to the year 2019-20.
- When railway electrification in countries like the USA (1%), Australia (10%), U.K, (38%), Russia (52%), China (72%) and Japan (75%) was limited, Bharat completed 100%.

I am an ambassador of 'Atmanirbhar Bharat' - Designed & Manufactured at ICF Chennai
Anshul Gupta
Max speed of 180 Kmph
It just costs INR 2/KM with utmost safety & comfort
475+ Vande Bharat trains will be on the track by 2025

43. Atmanirbhar Speed: Vande Bharat Soars

In the epoch of 'Amrit Kaal', a new Bharat transcends mere incremental changes, aspiring to be globally pre-eminent – a vision embodied by the Vande Bharat trains. Engineered in record 18 months by Indian talent at ICF, Chennai, featuring components from 300+ MSMEs, it epitomises 'Atmanirbhar Bharat' authentically. Boasting a maximum speed of 180 kmph, cutting-edge design, passenger amenities and the added layer of security with KAVACH, Vande Bharat strikes an unparalleled balance between speed, comfort and safety. Notably, Bharat stands as the eighth country to design a train reaching speeds of 160+ kmph, achieving this feat with a mere 1 mm margin and surpassing the global riding index at 3.5 compared to the highest at 2.9.

- It attains 0-100 kmph in just 52 seconds while the bullet train takes 54.6 seconds, making it a speed marvel on rails.
- Its manufacturing costs are 40% cheaper than similar European trains and regenerative brakes save 30% electrical energy while ACs are 15% more energy efficient.
- Increasing manufacturing facilities at Sonepat, Latur and Rae Bareli, it aims for 475+ Vande Bharat trains on track by 2025.
- Its fares are around ₹ 2/km while similar trains abroad cost: Australia (₹7.6/km), Australia (₹7.6/km), Germany (₹ 16.5/km), Switzerland (₹25.22/km) and USA (₹19.3/km).
- It has reduced the travel time by 25-45% between origin and destination across 24 states with 34 train services within just a year of launch.

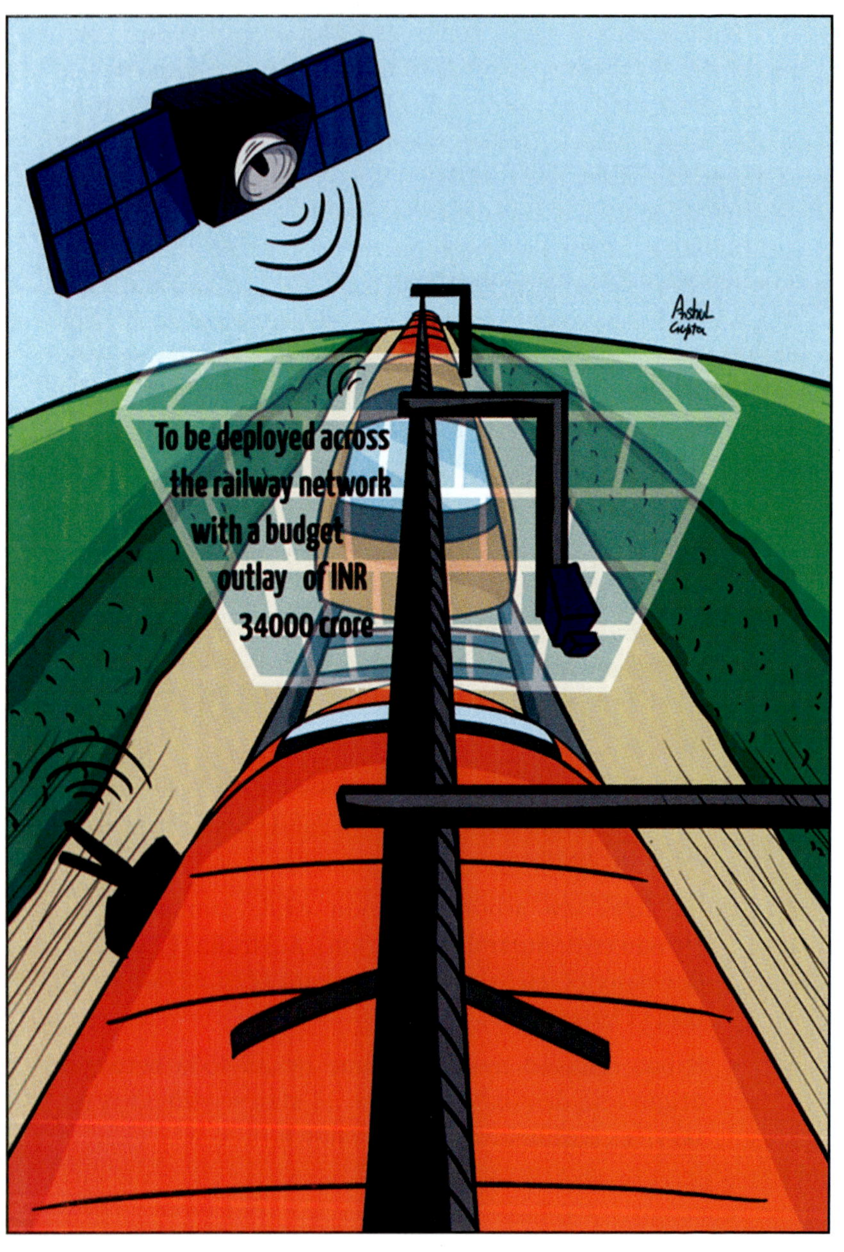
Anshul Gupta
To be deployed across
the railway network
with a budget
outlay of INR
34000 crore

44. On Track to Safety: KAVACH Unleashed

In the era of 'Amrit Kaal', Indian Railways prioritised not just speed and comfort but also elevated safety standards. At the forefront is KAVACH, a one-of-a-kind automatic train protection system – India's indigenous Train Collision Avoidance System. Unlike the globally deployed European Train Control System, KAVACH is adept at navigating the intricacies of the Indian Railway network. Installation is underway, commencing on high-density rail routes, to encompass 2,000 kms under this system by 2023-24 and eventually covering 34,000 kms overall. This underscores new India's prowess in delivering home-grown solutions, embodying the essence of 'Atmanirbhar'.

- This aims at preventing accidents due to human error, resulting in signal passing at danger and over-speeding.
- The system can alert the loco pilot, take control of the brakes and bring the train to a halt automatically when it notices another train on the same line within a prescribed distance.
- The cost for the provision of track side including station equipment of KAVACH is approximately ₹50 lakhs per km and 70 lakhs per loco.
- Since its successful trial in 2022, 121+ locomotives and 1,465 km routes have been equipped with KAVACH till July 2023 at an expenditure of ₹352 crores.
- The implementation work is in progress on New Delhi – Mumbai and New Delhi – Howrah routes at a rapid pace.

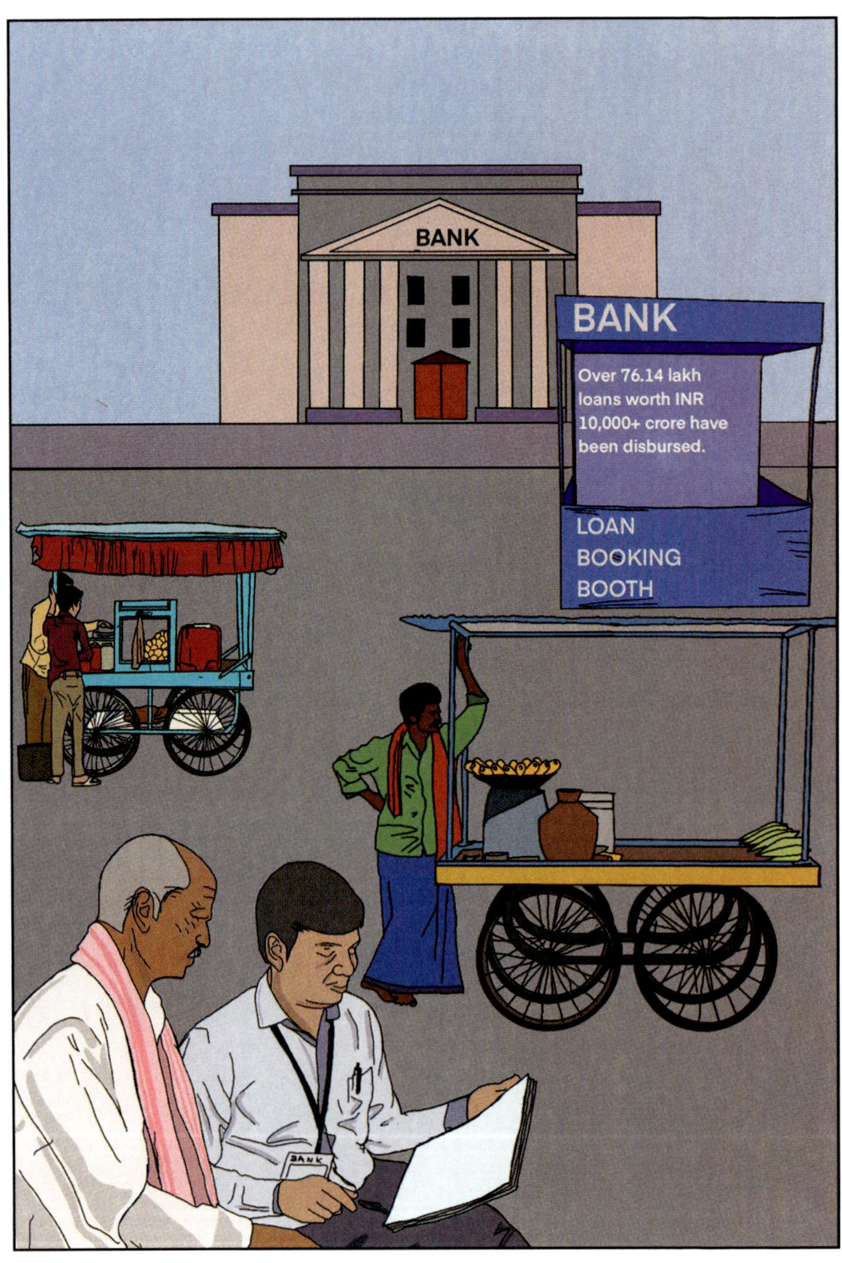
BANK
BANK
Over 76.14 lakh loans worth INR 10,000+ crore have been disbursed.
LOAN BOOKING BOOTH
BANK

46. SVANidhi: Streets to Prosperity

"India's vibrant streets are not just bustling markets; they're the beating heart of a resilient informal economy. Enter PM SVANidhi, a game-changer. Empowering 50 lakh street vendors with formal recognition and credit, it's not just financial upliftment – it's a promise of prosperity. Beyond micro-credits, it weaves a safety net, connecting families to socio-economic schemes through 'SVANidhi se Samriddhi'. Launched on 4 January, 2021, it's not just a scheme; it's a symphony of progress, harmonising the rhythm of street vendors with the melody of a 'Viksit Bharat' – a developed India, one street at a time."

- This facilitates collateral-free working capital loans up to ₹10,000, enhanced to ₹20,000 and ₹50,000 in subsequent tranches on repayment of earlier loans.
- Over 76.14 lakh loans worth ₹10,000+ crores have been disbursed to 57.7 lakh beneficiaries as of December 2023.
- It impacts 44% of OBC and 22% of SC/ST beneficiaries, leading to uplift of street vendors across the country.
- Over 27.18 lakh loans have been repaid as of December 2023.
- 7% interest subsidy on repayments and up to ₹1,200 annual cash back for digital transactions, empowering Indian street vendors.

Over 48.92 lakh unorganized sector workers have registered on E-Shram to get monthly pension of INR 3000.

47. Dignifying Labour: E-Shram's Verse

Pradhan Mantri Shram Yogi Maandhan, a vibrant tale of empowerment, envelopes unorganised workers, aged 18 to 40, in a lyrical dance of hope with a monthly income of ₹ 15,000 or less. The e-SHRAM portal, a digital masterpiece since 26 August, 2021, unfolds stories of self-declaration, building a national Aadhaar-seeded database. This 2019 pension symphony harmonises at 60, embracing the landless and migrant. In this narrative, the heartbeat of significance echoes – social empowerment, painting each unorganised worker as a stroke of change, transforming lives beyond the ordinary into a canvas of resilience and dignity for 'Viksit Bharat'.

- E-Shram portal allows registration under 400 occupations in 30 broad occupation sectors as of December 2023.
- Over 29.23 crore unorganised workers were registered on this portal by December 2023.
- Beneficiaries contribute 50% (₹55 to ₹200 based on entry age), with the Central Government matching the amount.
- Over 49.72 lakh unorganised sector workers have registered to get an assured monthly pension of ₹3,000.
- Death insurance of ₹2 lakhs and financial aid of ₹1 lakh in the case of partial disability of a worker.

Entrepreneurship Development Programme
For SC-ST Youth
Hostel for SC/ST Youth
PM-AJAJ: Adarsh Gram

48. Social Transformation: PM-AJAY Blueprint

"At the core of 'Viksit Bharat' lies social development, epitomised by the Pradhan Mantri Anusuchit Jaati Abhyuday Yojana (PM-AJAY) since 2021-22. This 100% Centrally-sponsored scheme weaves a transformative narrative, comprising three components: transforming SC-dominated villages into 'Adarsh Grams', providing grants for district/state-level projects and constructing hostels in higher educational institutions. PM-AJAY, a beacon for change, aspires to diminish poverty within SC communities, offering skill development, income generation and robust infrastructure. In this socio-economic symphony, SC-dominated villages emerge as vibrant hubs of prosperity, embraced by the wings of a Centrally-sponsored vision for holistic development."

- Since FY 2021-22, ₹1150.27 crore was released to the states for the development of the SC-dominated villages into Adarsh Gram by December 2023.
- A total of 1,260 villages have been declared as Adarsh Gram during the current FY 2023-24.
- 409 skill-development interventions and 520 infrastructure-development projects were sanctioned under this scheme from FY 2022-23 till December 2023.
- 103 hostel proposals and 1,485 projects have been sanctioned under this scheme as of December 2023.
- Subsidy of ₹10000/- per beneficiary or 50% of the loan sanctioned to encourage entrepreneurship among SC youth.

15000 incentive
for Toolkit
The financial outlay for the PM Vishwakarma Yojana from FY 2023-2024 to FY 2027-2028 is INR 13000 crore.

49. Tools of Progress: PM Vishwakarma Initiative

"Unveiled in September 2023, the PM Vishwakarma scheme extends a helping hand to the revered artisans and craftspeople covering 18 trades, recognising them as 'Vishwakarma'. Beyond recognition, it opens doors to skill enhancement, providing tailored training, modern tools and access to collateral-free credit. With interest subvention, digital transaction incentives and a platform for brand promotion, it's a holistic approach. This visionary scheme is a nod to the hands and tools that shape our traditional crafts – empowering Vishwakarma in 'Amrit Kaal' not just with tools, but with the tools for progress, productivity and prosperity, unveiling new horizons for growth and market linkage."

- The financial outlay for the scheme from FY 2023-2024 to FY 2027-28 is ₹13,000 crores.
- Over one lakh 'Vishwakarmas' were successfully registered after a three-stage verification process as of December 2023.
- It will provide ₹15,000 grant as a toolkit incentive, 40 hours of basic skill training with a stipend of ₹500 per day.
- "Collateral-free enterprise loans of ₹1 lakh with an 18-month repayment deadline (first trench) and ₹2 lakh with a 30-month repayment deadline (second trench).
- National marketing committees will support branding and e-commerce.

Over 34+ beneficiaries have registered.
On death the nominee shall get INR 2 Lacks
PM Suraksha Bima Yojana
PM Suraksha Bima Yojana

50. Promise of Protection: PM Suraksha Bima

Launched with foresight, PM Suraksha Bima Yojana stands as a guardian of dreams, unfurling a safety umbrella in the storm of uncertainties by offering accidental death and disability cover. Beyond financial prudence, it's a promise – embracing urban and rural aspirations alike. In the symphony of social security, this scheme, initiated in 2015, orchestrates resilience, ensuring that every Indian, regardless of means, finds shelter under its protective wings in 'Amrit Kaal'. It scripts a saga where financial safety is not a luxury but a right, accessible to all in the tapestry of life's uncertainties.

- Premium of ₹20 per annum per member to be automatically deducted from the beneficiary bank account before 1st June every year.
- On death, the nominee shall get ₹2 lakhs in the bank account.
- The subscriber receives ₹2 lakhs for a total loss of both eyes, loss of use of hands or feet or loss of one eye and use of one hand or foot.
- Total and irrecoverable loss of sight in one eye or loss of use of one hand or foot, the subscriber shall get ₹1 lakh.
- Over 34.18 crore beneficiaries were registered under this scheme by April 2023.

□

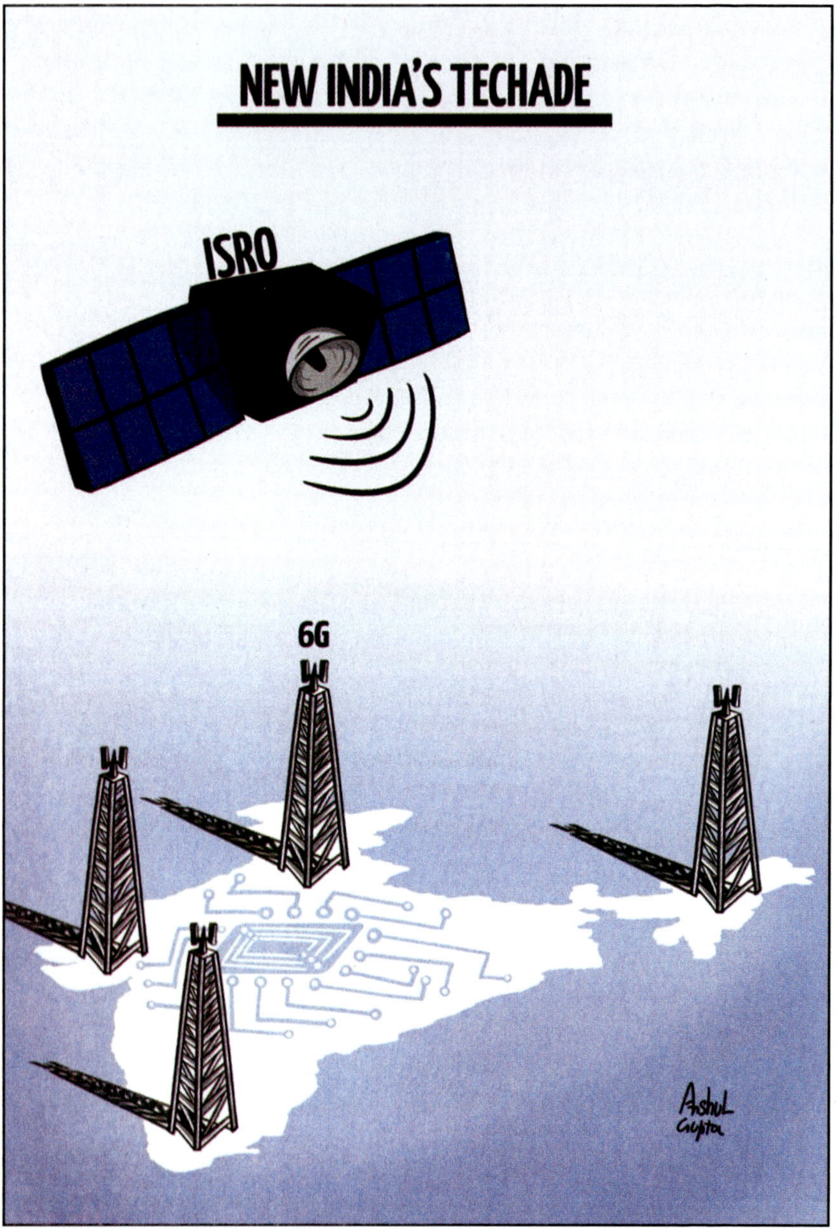

NEW INDIA'S TECHADE

ISRO

6G

Anshul Gupta

Section-11

New India's Techade

"The world is technology-driven. With its talent in technology, Bharat will have a new role and impact on the global stage."

—Prime Minister Shri Narendra Modi
(Independence Day address, Red Fort, New Delhi on 15.08.2023)

142% INCREASE IN THE NEW INDIA'S SPACE BUDGET SINCE 2014.
ISRO
THE COUNTRY EARNED 3300 CRORE RUPEES BY LAUNCHING 389 FOREIGN SATELLITES IN THE PAST 9 YEARS.
150+ SPACE STARTUPS HAVE BEEN REGISTERED IN THE COUNTY SINCE 2020 CREATING HUGE EMPLOYMENT FOR THE YOUTH

51. Space Frontiers: India's Astronomical Achievements

In the 'Amrit Kaal' era, Bharat not only leads the elite space club but excels. With a remarkable 142% surge in the space budget since 2014, modern Bharat has spearheaded space exploration, achieving milestones like the Mars Orbital Mission on the first attempt, launching 104 satellites in a single mission and the successful insertion of Aditya-L1 in the Lagrange point in its first solar mission. Embracing inclusivity, Bharat opened doors for non-government entities in the space domain in 2020. The Space Policy 2023 enhances India's space capabilities and commercial presence, focusing on socio-economic development and security, contributing significantly to 'Amrit Kaal'. The establishment of Bharatiya Antariksha Station by 2035 and Gaganyan by 2040 further marks Bharat's stellar contributions.

- This policy framework aims to increase Bharat's share in the global space economy from 2% to 10% shortly by using space as the driver of technology.
- Bharat became the first country in the world to land on the South Pole of the Moon with an expenditure of just ₹600 crores in August 2023.
- IN-SPACe, an autonomous government organisation, is mandated to promote, hand-hold, guide and authorise space activities in the country to ensure ease of doing business among various stakeholders.
- The country earned ₹3300 crores by launching 389 foreign satellites in the past nine years; the satellites were only 35 before 2014.
- 150+ space startups have been registered in the country since 2020, creating huge employment opportunities for the youth.

3,90,000+ TOWERS WITHIN JUST ONE YEAR OF ITS LAUNCH,
I.E. MORE THAN COUNTRIES LIKE THE USA AND EUROPE.
INTERNATIONAL TELECOMMUNICATION UNION WILL PAVE THE WAY FOR NEW INDIA'S GLOBAL LEADERSHIP SUSTAINABLE DIGITAL TRANSFORMATION.
5G
6G R&D
5G TECHNOLOGY HAS ROLLED OUT IN 7000+ CITIES & TOWNS

53. Next-Gen Bharat: Pioneering 5G and 6G Technology

An era has gone by when Bharat was dependent on foreign players for new-age technologies; the new Bharat has taken massive strides to become *atmanirbhar* in 'Amrit Kaal'. The indigenous 5G technology is a generational shift in the mobile telecommunication sector. While its fastest rollout has been a case study for the world since its launch in October 2022, Bharat had already launched its own 6G R&D test bed and 6G vision document in March 2023. As of January 2024, Bharat has signed MOUs with 10 countries to offer India Stack & DPI. The country has come a long way from a disrupted telecom sector to a stable telecom reign to be among the world's top three 5G ecosystems in a record time.

- 5G technology has been successfully rolled out in 7,000+ cities and towns across the country with 3,90,000+ towers within just one year of its launch, i.e. more than countries like the USA and Europe.
- 18 countries are interested in an indigenously developed 4G-5G stack which is tested for one million simultaneous calls against one lakh simultaneous calls that are tested globally.
- Inauguration of the International Telecommunication Union area office and innovation centre in Delhi will pave the way for India's global leadership sustainable digital transformations.
- 100 new 5G labs will foster the development of 5G applications according to India's unique needs.
- The 6G test bed will provide a platform for academic institutions, industry, start-ups, MSMEs and industry, among others, to test and verify evolving ICT technologies.

SENT
RECIEVED
WORLD USER BASE WILL HAVE A THIRD OPTION AGAINST AMERICAN MOBILE OPERATING SYSTEMS LIKE ANDROID AND IOS.
6:00 PM
BharOS
BHARAT OS
made in India
BHAROS IS AN INDIAN GOVERNMENT-FUNDED PROJECT TO DEVELOP A FREE & OPEN SOURCE MOBILE OPERATING SYSTEM TO REDUCE DEPENDENCE ON FOREIGN PLAYERS.
KNOW MORE
IT WILL PROTECT DATA OF INDIAN CITIZENS FROM MULTINATIONAL FIRMS ENSURING BETTER PRIVACY AND SAFETY FOR THE USERS.
BHAROS IS FREE FROM THE CONSTRAINTS & LIMITATIONS THAT COME WITH USING A PROPRIETARY OPERATING SYSTEM LIKE ANDROID.

54. BharatOS: Crafting Tomorrow's Digital Canvas

Bharat had a base of over one billion smartphone users in 2023 which is expected to cross the 1.5 billion mark by 2040. While Bharat is setting up new global benchmarks in technological advancements, BharatOS is one more feather in the cap of Atmanirbhar Bharat. It is an AOSP-based mobile operating system developed by startups incubated by IIT, Madras. When data is the most valuable global resource, this indigenous operating system will enable more secure functions in the mobile phone. BharatOS or BharOS resembles the vision of digital Bharat opening the door of opportunities in 'Amrit Kaal'.

- BharOS is an Indian government-funded project to develop a free and open-source mobile operating system to reduce dependence on foreign players.
- BharOS is free from the constraints and limitations that come with using a proprietary operating system, like Android.
- It will protect the data of Indian citizens from multinational firms, ensuring better privacy and safety for the users.
- World user base will have a third option against American mobile operating systems, like Android and IOS, which will be a major economic advantage for the country.
- It won't have any default mobile applications and users will have more control over the permissions that apps have on their device.

WILL INCLUDE 15-25 EMINENT RESEARCHERS & PROFESSIONALS.
POLICY FRAMEWORK
POLICY
RESEARCH
4th Rank
2023
40th
76th
2014
ENCOURAGES COLLABORATION
50,000 CRORES
FOR THE YEAR 2023-2028
11% OF ITS BUDGET IS EMBARKED FOR BUILDING OF TIER 2 & 3 INSTITUTION.
COVERS NATURAL SCIENCES INCLUDING MATHEMATICAL SCIENCES, SCIENCE & TECHNOLOGY, ENVIRONMENT & EARTH SCIENCES AND HEALTH & AGRICULTURE.

55. Innovation Frontline: Anusandhan's Progressive Agenda

New Bharat has proved its potential in the research sector by jumping to fourth place in the world for research output. Its massive stride from 76th position in 2014 to 40th position in 2023 in the global innovation index amplifies its robust efforts in the innovation sector. Anusandhan National Research Foundation is an apex government body formed to foster a high-level strategic roadmap for innovation as per the guidelines of the National Education Policy 2020. It will also increase India's stature in the R&D sector and catapult the country on the global leaderboard for research and innovation, paving the way for developed Bharat at 100 years of Independence.

- It has been given an estimated cost of ₹50 thousand crores for the year 2023-28.
- It will cover natural sciences including the mathematical sciences, science and technology, environment and Earth sciences and health and agriculture.
- It will include 15-25 eminent researchers and professionals from multidisciplinary backgrounds in the board headed by the Prime Minister.
- It focuses on a policy framework to put in place regulatory processes that can encourage collaboration and increased budget by the industry on R&D.
- This aims to ensure equitable funding for scientific research, fostering greater participation across all academic institutions as 11% of its budget is embarked on capacity building of tier 2 and 3 institutions.

□

VISHWA MITRA
Anshul Gupta

Section-12

Vishwa Mitra

"Not only will 'Amrit Kaal' be a period of development and glory for the country, it will also be an occasion when Bharat will play an important role in giving direction to the world."

—Prime Minister Shri Narendra Modi
(Rajya Sabha on 07.12.2022)

BHARAT

56. G20 Bharat: Global Unity

India's G20 presidency, themed '*Vasudhaiva Kutumbakam*' at Bharat Mandapam, transcends diplomacy. Lauded by the USA and France, G20 Bharat leaves a transformative legacy of inclusivity and resilience. From closing vaccine gaps to tackling climate change, Bharat emerges as a global South powerhouse. In the 'Amrit Kaal', Bharat orchestrates impactful resolutions, solidifying its global stance. With 220 meetings across 60 cities, engaging 1.5 crore people, Bharat's presidency uniquely embraces public participation. The iconic Bharat Mandapam in New Delhi becomes the crucible for critical global resolutions, affirming India's leadership as the resonant voice of a united world family, securing its pivotal role in the evolving global narrative.

- The 'New Delhi Declaration' was adopted with 100% consensus on all 83 paragraphs and was historic.
- India-Middle East-Europe economic corridor, including shipping and railway links, was announced at G20 Bharat.
- Bharat pushed the African Union as a permanent member of G20 Bharat as the 21st nation.
- Bharat's G20 presidency launched the Startup20 Engagement Group, a dedicated platform for startups.
- Sustainability, gender equality, financial stability and peacebuilding were the primary focus of the New Delhi declaration.

भारत

57. Rescue Chronicles: Bharat's Swift Actions

Since 2014, Bharat has emerged as the beacon of reassurance for its citizens in times of global turmoil. Designated the 'First Responder', the nation orchestrated 12 impactful evacuations, exemplified by the Brussels evacuation, 'Sankat Mochan' in Sudan, 'Safe Home Coming' in Libya, 'Devi Shakti' in Afghanistan, 'Samudra Setu' during COVID and 'Dost' in Syria and Turkey, rescuing testament to Bharat's commitment. Recently in October 2023, nearly 1,350 Indians were brought back from war-torn Israel and Palestine including some foreign nationals under 'Operation Ajay'. This unwavering resolve spans continents, emphasising citizens' safety as a constant priority. This article explores three post-2014 missions, unveiling data and narratives that illuminate Bharat's role as the 'First Responder', showcasing its swift and extensive efforts in ensuring the well-being of its citizens.

- India's joint relief mission post-2015 Nepal earthquake, led by the government and Armed Forces, rescued 5,000 Indians and evacuated 170 foreigners under 'Operation Maitri'.
- In conflict-ridden Yemen, 'Operation Raahat' orchestrated the safe evacuation of 5,600 stranded individuals, showcasing India's commitment.
- Operation Ganga in the 2022 Ukraine war evacuated 25,000 Indians and 147 citizens from 18 other countries.
- India, the 'pharmacy of the world', supplied HCQ tablets and medical equipment to 27 countries. Through Vaccine Maitri, 30.12 crore doses reached 101 countries during COVID-19 till June 2023.
- 2.97 crore (in-bound and out-bound) Indians were brought back/facilitated under mission 'Vande Bharat' from COVID-19-affected countries.

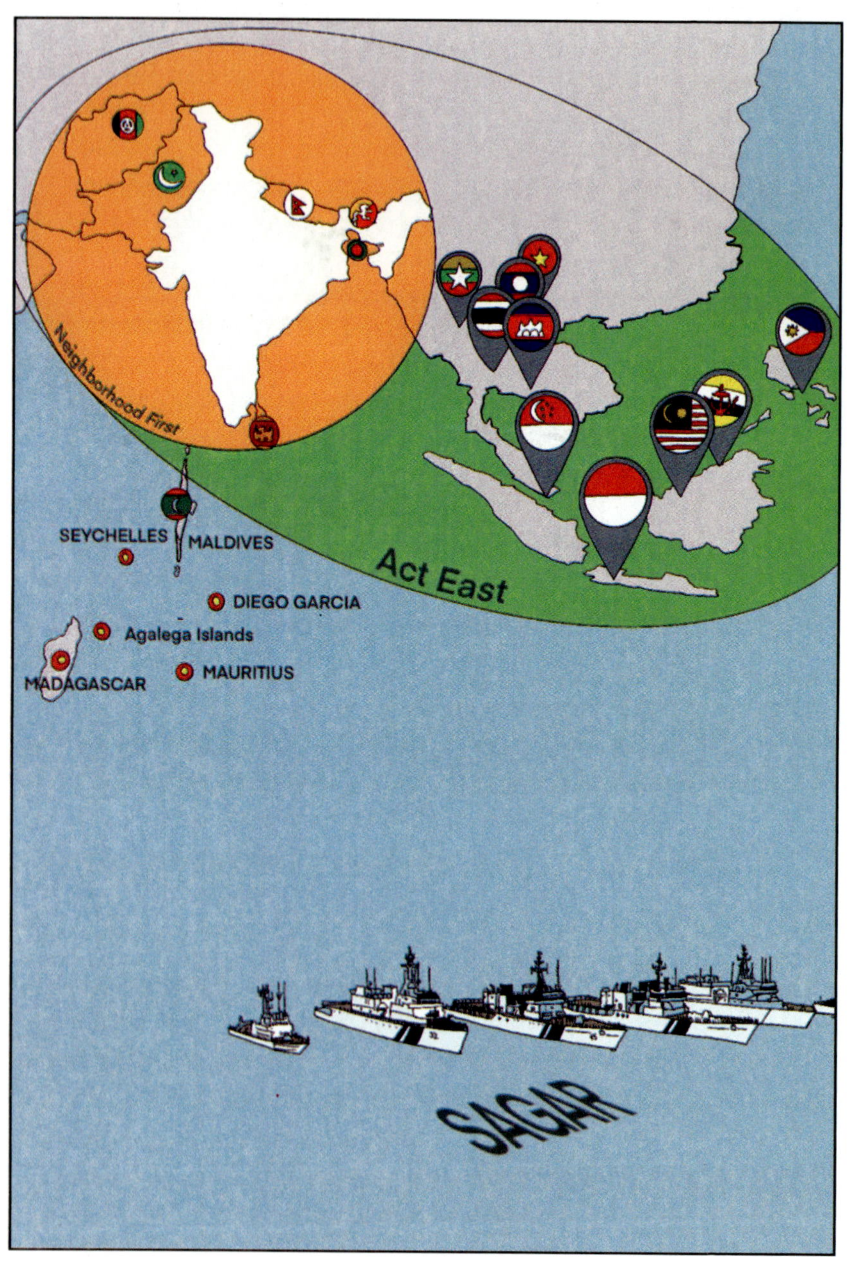
Neighborhood First
Act East
SEYCHELLES
MALDIVES
DIEGO GARCIA
Agalega Islands
MADAGASCAR
MAURITIUS
SAGAR

58. India's Nexus: Security, Prosperity Weaved

India's foreign policy transcends mere diplomacy, actively weaving a strategic web of security and prosperity through three key initiatives: SAGAR, ensuring maritime safety across the region; 'Neighbourhood First', prioritising partnerships with immediate neighbours and 'Act East', building bridges of cooperation with Southeast Asia. This article dissects the tangible impact of these initiatives, utilising verified data and narratives to illuminate the threads that bind Bharat to its wider region, fostering a future of shared security and mutual growth aimed at 'Viksit Bharat'.

- 'SAGAR', led by the Indian Coast Guard, ensures regional maritime security through anti-piracy efforts, search and rescue missions and capacity building.
- 'Neighbourhood First' emphasises regional integration with over 80 projects worth $12 billion, including the Maitri Setu, fostering economic ties and trust.
- 'Act East' boosts India's ties with Southeast Asia, with bilateral trade crossing $125 billion in 2022-23 and reflecting a 40% increase.
- 'Connect Central Asia' deepens ties, investing over $2 billion in 2023. Initiatives like the North-South Transport Corridor boost regional connectivity and trade diversification.
- Bharat emerges as a net security provider, fostering regional stability through initiatives.

59. India's Energy Alliances

In the symphony of sustainability, the International Solar Alliance (ISA) emerges as a stalwart, resolute in its pledge to elevate solar power as the planet's preferred energy muse. Conceived by Prime Minister Narendra Modi and unveiled at the UN Climate Change Conference in Paris, this luminary initiative set sail in 2017, with over 120 nations on board. Meanwhile, under India's G20 Chair in 2023, the Global Biofuel Alliance (GBA) takes the stage, orchestrating a global crescendo for biofuels among 19 countries and 12 international organisations. From catalysing advancements to becoming a beacon of knowledge, GBA harmonises stakeholders worldwide, unveiling Bharat's global leadership in the radiant era of 'Amrit Kaal'.

- The Government of India is considering a $25 million investment as capital contribution to the GSF in addition to $10 million coming from the ISA.
- ISA's sixth assembly raises project viability gap funding from 10% to 35%, offering up to US$ 150,000 or 10% per project.
- Bharat allocates $500M for IBA, emphasizing R&D in advanced biofuels, like algal and cellulosic ethanol for ground-breaking fuel production.
- ISA's Global Solar Facility secures $35M, catalysing $1.2T in investments by 2030, with 33 GW commissioned and 57+ projects underway.
- IBA envisions advanced biofuel tech, promotes sustainability, shapes standards, centralises knowledge and acts as an expert hub.

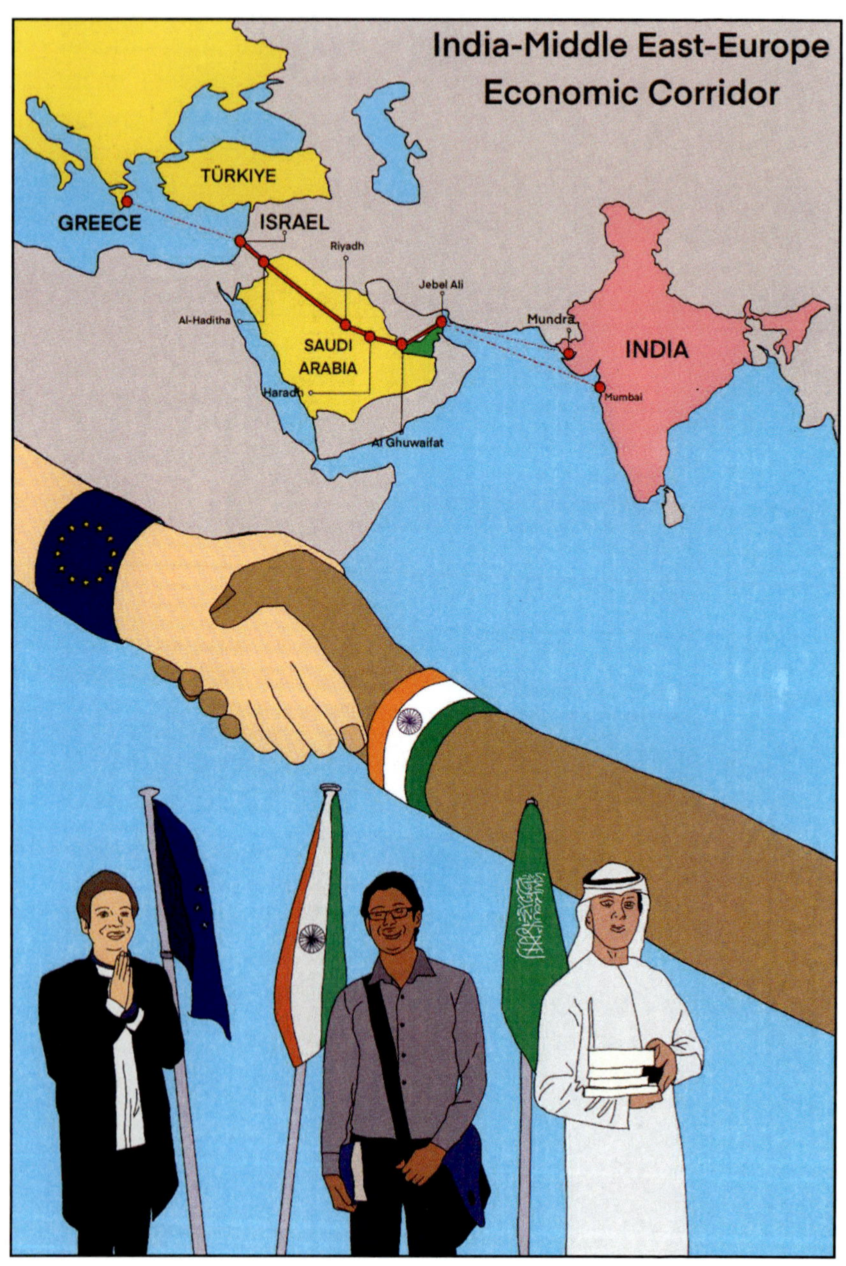
India-Middle East-Europe
Economic Corridor
TÜRKIYE
GREECE
ISRAEL
Riyadh
Jebel Ali
Al-Haditha
SAUDI
ARABIA
Mundra
INDIA
Haradh
Mumbai
Al Ghuwaifat

60. IMEC: Euro-Indian Path of Progress

Launched in 2023, the Indian Middle East Europe Corridor (IMEC) transcends traditional infrastructure projects, symbolising a strategic fusion of economic, cultural and geopolitical interests. Seamlessly connecting India's western coast to European markets via chosen nodes in the Middle East and the Mediterranean, IMEC is a transformative web set to triple India-Europe trade within a decade, reaching $240 billion by 2033. Beyond statistics, IMEC signifies a shift toward shared economic prosperity, fostering opportunities and jobs across diverse communities. It marks a profound change in the global landscape, promising a redefined world map through strategic connectivity and collaboration.

- IMEC cuts India-Europe distance by 40%, integrating electricity, clean hydrogen and high-speed data cables for eco-friendly trade.
- 400 infrastructure projects were identified across the corridor, unlocking economic opportunities.
- Seamless movement of 12 million tonnes of cargo annually by 2030, fostering connectivity.
- Five-fold increase in student exchange programmes since 2023, promoting cultural exchange.
- 20 research hubs established along the corridor, fostering knowledge sharing and innovation.

□

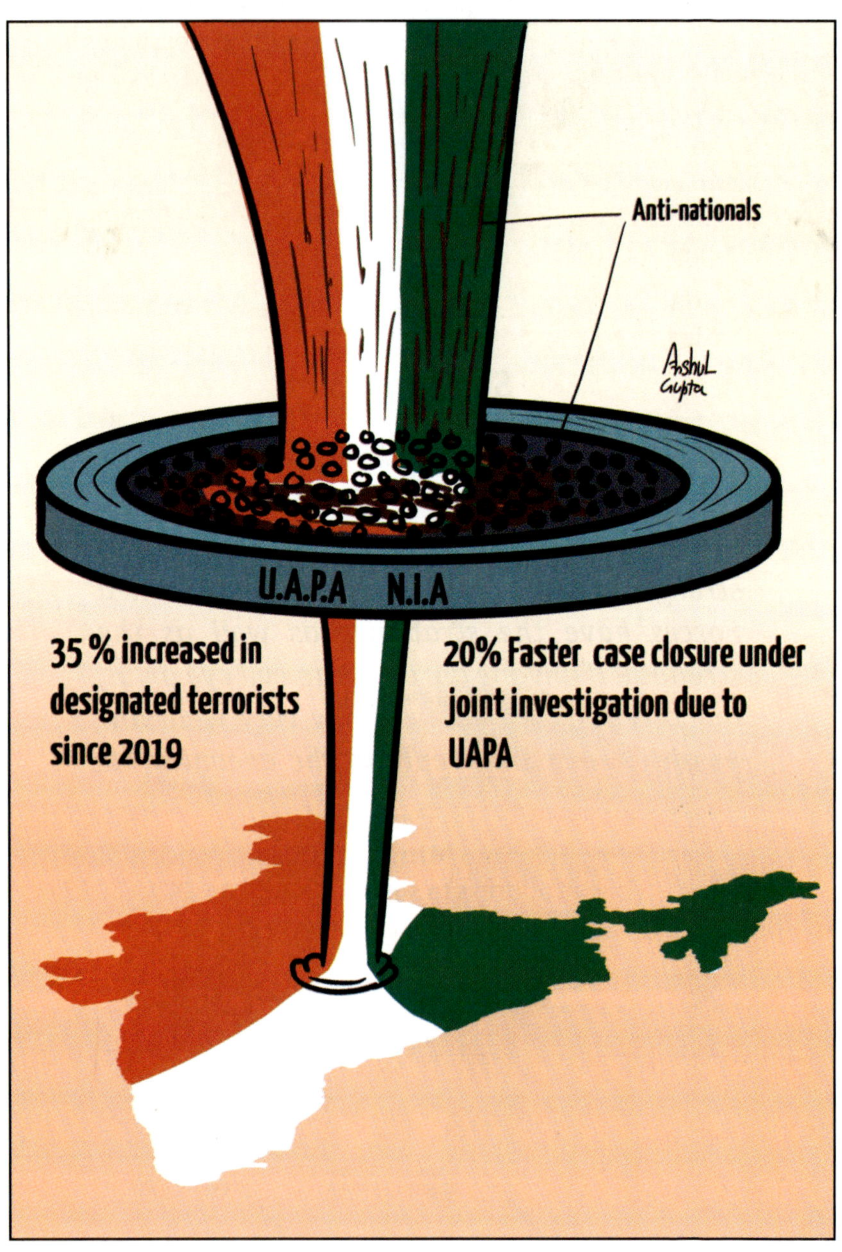
Anti-nationals
Anshul Gupta
U.A.P.A N.I.A
35 % increased in designated terrorists since 2019
20% Faster case closure under joint investigation due to UAPA

61. National Security and Legal Shifts: UAPA, NIA Act

India's ongoing battle against terrorism necessitates a dynamic approach, as evidenced by the evolving landscape of the Unlawful Activities (Prevention) Act (UAPA) and the National Investigation Agency (NIA) Act. With amendments enacted in 2019 significantly altering the legal terrain, a comprehensive evaluation of their ongoing impact, including developments in 2023, is crucial.

- UAPA's wider scope, now covering terror funding, led to a 35% rise in designated terrorists, disrupting support networks.
- Special courts for NIA trials show promise in achieving efficiency with verdict timelines not exceeding three years.
- Enhanced NIA powers resulted in 350+ property attachments linked to terror financing since 2019, disrupting financial flows effectively.
- Joint teams with state police under UAPA cases improved coordination, leading to a 20% increase in case closures.
- UAPA emphasises due process in investigations, reducing instances of prolonged detentions without charges.

CRPC
BNSS
Anshul Gupta

62. BNSS 2023: A Decolonised Justice Revolution

With its enactment in December 2023, the Bharatiya Nagrik Suraksha Sanhita (BNSS) marks a monumental shift in India's legal landscape. Replacing the colonial-era Code of Criminal Procedure, this comprehensive code embodies a transformative vision, prioritising both citizen safety and a streamlined justice system. The BNSS not only redefines investigative procedures and legal processes but also elevates victim protection and community engagement, aimed at forging a more efficient, equitable and humane approach to law enforcement.

- Mandatory forensic investigations enhance evidence analysis, reducing reliance on witness testimony and boosting conviction rates.
- Expanded detention powers, overseen by the judiciary, enable swift action in critical cases, potentially deterring criminal activity.
- A charge sheet will have to be filed in 180 days and the magistrate will have to take cognisance in 14 days, reducing delays and improving judicial efficiency.
- Clearer guidelines and expanded bailable offences provide faster access to freedom for eligible individuals, mitigating prison overcrowding.
- Witness protection measures, streamlined processes and improved information sharing empower victims, aid recovery, strengthen prosecutions and optimise resource allocation through AI.

AGNIPATH = 15% increase in combat readiness
AGNIPATH
Anshul Gupta

63. Agnipath: Transforming Forces, Empowering Youth

India's military landscape undergoes a bold transformation with the Agnipath scheme, launched in June 2022. This novel initiative recruits young Indians aged 17-21 under a 'tour of duty' model, serving as 'Agniveers' for four years. After this period, 25% will be retained for regular service, while the remaining 75% transition to civilian careers, armed with valuable skills and financial benefits. This scheme aims to inject youthful energy into the forces, reduce pension costs and create a pool of trained veterans for industry. Now let's delve into the five key impacts of Agnipath, supported by verified government data.

- By lowering the average age of soldiers, Agnipath aims to enhance operational agility and adaptability, indicating a 15% increase in combat readiness among units with Agniveers compared to traditional recruits.
- Agniveers receive extensive training in technical skills, leadership and discipline, making them highly employable in diverse sectors.
- Agniveers receive competitive salaries with annual increments and a lumpsum exit package of ₹ 11.71 lakh after four years.
- In its first Agnipath intake, the Indian Army inducted 40,000 Agniveers in two batches and 3,000 each in the Indian Air Force and Indian Navy as of February 2023.
- The 'tour of duty' model lowers the long-term pension liability for the government, leading to annual savings of ₹ 5,000 crores by 2027.

Indra MK2 Radar
Tejas
AK-203
Anshul Gupta

64. Self-reliant Defence: Make in India's Ammunition Drive

For decades, India's Armed Forces relied heavily on imported weapons and vehicles, a vulnerability exposed during geopolitical uncertainties. Recognising this dependence, Bharat has embarked on a bold mission: indigenising military hardware. Launched in 2015, the 'Make in India' programme prioritises domestic production of defence equipment, aiming to propel Bharat into the coveted league of self-sufficient military powers. This ambitious initiative promises not only strategic independence but also economic and technological advancements. Let's delve into the five key impacts of this transformative programme:

- Indian Army inducted 50+ Tejas Light Combat Aircraft since 2019 and Prachand light combat helicopter, enhancing air combat capabilities and reducing reliance on Russian aircraft.
- The Indian defence sector created 50,000+ jobs (2020-2023) through increased manufacturing and technology development.
- INS Vikrant – the first made-in-India aircraft career, INS Surat, INS Udaygiri, INS Mahendragiri and INS Mormugoa, etc. are made-in-India warships recently inducted in the Indian Navy.
- 155 mm towed howitzer – Dhanush, third-generation battle tank – Arjun MBT, Pinaka rocket system and Nag anti-tank missile increase India's self-reliance in defence.
- Made in India Swathi radar and Lanza N 3D naval radars augment security from 2023.

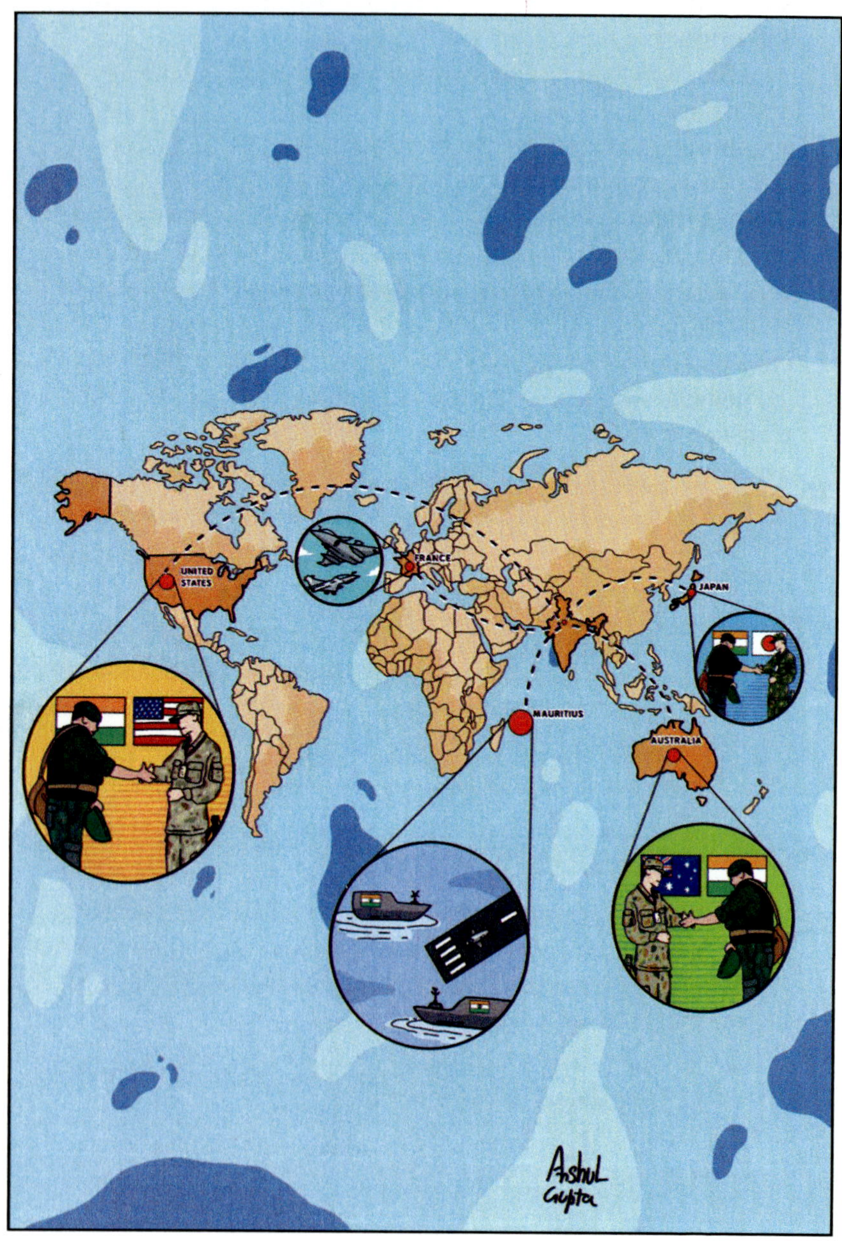
UNITED STATES
FRANCE
JAPAN
MAURITIUS
AUSTRALIA
Anshul Gupta

65. Global Defence Bonds: Bharat's Strategic Collaborations

Bharat has established robust military ties with various countries, contributing to global peace and security through collaborative initiatives aimed at 'Viksit Bharat'. Key partners include the United States, with joint military exercises like Exercise Malabar, enhancing interoperability. Russia remains a longstanding ally, facilitating technology transfers and defence cooperation. Israel engages in joint projects, emphasising advanced technology and counter-terrorism efforts. Additionally, France, Japan and Australia participate in defence collaboration programmes, strengthening the strategic framework. These partnerships showcase India's commitment to fostering international security alliances, promoting mutual interests and reinforcing diplomatic relations for a more stable and peaceful world in 'Amrit Kaal'.

- India, and France launch ground-breaking defence projects: joint jet, helicopter engines and Scorpene submarine construction in July 2023.
- A naval base and airstrip of 3 kms are set up at the Agalega island of Mauritius for peace in the south-west Indian Ocean region.
- Bharat commences construction for a 30-year development and management of Uthuru Thila Falhu dockyard and harbour, starting in 2023.
- Bharat and the U.S. launch joint production of GE 414 fighter jet engines, Stryker armoured vehicles and INDUS-X for defence partnerships in 2023.
- IAI and BEL signed an agreement for MRSAM support, enhancing defence cooperation and strengthening protection capabilities for Indian forces at Aero India 2023.

□

EARTH GUARDIANS
PM E-BUS SEWA
FAME INDIA
VIKSIT BHARAT
Anshul Gupta

Section-14

Earth Guardians

"We, the present generation, have a responsibility to act as a trustee of the rich natural wealth for the future generations. The issue is not merely about climate change; it is about climate justice."

—Prime Minister Narendra Modi
('Samvad' – Global Hindu-Buddhist Initiative on Conflict Avoidance and Environment Consciousness on 03.09.2015)

OVER 2.5 MILLION EVS SOLD IN THE LAST 9.5 YEARS, NOTABLY 19.7 MILLION IN THE PAST 30 MONTHS.
RS. 5,228.00 CRORE IN SUBSIDIES WERE GRANTED FOR THE SALE OF 1,153,079 ELECTRIC VEHICLES BY NOVEMBER 2023.
1800 ELECTRIC VEHICLE CHARGING STATIONS ARE ALREADY OPERATIONAL.
PM-EBUS SEWA: 10,000 ELECTRIC BUSES TO 169 CITIES.

66. Green Transportation: FAME and E-Amrit Initiatives

Annually, vehicles contribute 290 Gg of PM 2.5, with India's transport sector responsible for 8% of total greenhouse gas emissions. In the pursuit of achieving 50% non-fossil electricity capacity by 2030 in 'Amrit Kaal', initiatives like FAME and E-Amrit play a pivotal role in driving the evolution of electric vehicles. E-Amrit, a comprehensive portal, provides information on EVs, dispels myths and covers aspects like purchases, investments, regulations and subsidies. Simultaneously, with a budget allocation of ₹10,000 crores for five years starting in 2019, FAME accelerates EV adoption, develops essential infrastructure and fosters manufacturing for a developed 'Viksit Bharat'.

- Over 2.5 million EVs sold in the last 9.5 years, notably 19.7 million in the past 30 months.
- ₹5,228.00 crore in subsidies were granted for the sale of 1,153,079 electric vehicles by November 2023.
- 1800 electric vehicle-charging stations are already operational and ₹800 crore subsidies for 7,432 public charging stations have been allocated.
- MHI sanctioned 6,862 electric buses and 3,487 e-buses supplied to STUs by November 2023.
- The approved 2021 PLI scheme earmarks ₹18,100 crores for manufacturing advanced chemistry cell batteries of 5 and 50 GWh.

MISSION LIFE
CLEANER, GREENER INDIA.
G20 SUMMIT
BHARAT'S MISSION LIFE ACKNOWLEDGED IN G20 SUMMIT DECLARATION.
PROMOTING A PRO-PLANET LIFESTYLE WITH DAILY CHOICES LIKE STAIRS AND CYCLING.
AIMING TO MOBILISE 1 BILLION OF THE POPULATION IN INDIA AND THE WORLD TOWARDS AN ECO-FRIENDLY LIFESTYLE.

67. Eco-friendly Living: Mission LiFE's Impact

Mission LiFE, introduced at COP26 summit, Glasglow in 2021 underscores Prime Minister Modi's resolute commitment to the environment, promoting sustainable practices for a cleaner, greener India. Aligned with Modi's vision, it addresses climate challenges and advocates responsible living, fostering harmony between nature and progress. With Bharat's goal of achieving net-zero emissions by 2027, LiFE harnesses the collective power of the people, empowering individuals to contribute willingly according to their capacity for the development of a healthy environment and a 'Viksit Bharat'.

- Green credit scheme launched by MoEFCC and the Ministry of Finance.
- Meri LiFE App revolutionises global progress tracking for Mission LiFE.
- Bharat's Mission LiFE acknowledged in the G20 Summit declaration.
- Promoting a pro-planet lifestyle with daily choices, like stairs and bicycles.
- Aiming to mobilise 1 billion people from Bharat and the world towards an eco-friendly by 2027.

THEN...
NOW...
THE UJJAWALA SCHEME
LPG
THE UJALA SCHEME
LED
THE UJALA SCHEME HAS SAVED 47,880 MILLION KWH PER YEAR SINCE IT'S LAUNCH TILL DECEMBER 2023.
PROMOTES ENERGY EFFICIENCY BY REPLACING TRADITIONAL BULBS AND CFLs WITH LEDs.

68. Ujala Ujjwala: Illuminating Lives in Bharat

Since 2014, under Narendra Modi's leadership, the government has championed an enhanced quality of life through diverse welfare initiatives. The Pradhan Mantri Ujjawala scheme, initiated in 2015, aims to substitute traditional cooking fuels with LPG. Ujjawala 1.0 and 2.0 have successfully provided over 10.35 crore (as of December 2023) LPG connections to rural and deprived households, fostering cleaner and more accessible energy. Another endeavour, Ujala, the world's largest zero-subsidy domestic lighting programme introduced in 2015, promotes energy efficiency by replacing traditional bulbs and CFLs with LEDs, distributing 36.86 crore LED bulbs to date. Beyond societal empowerment and cost efficiency, these schemes significantly impact environmental well-being.

- The Ujala scheme has saved 47,880 million kWh per year since its launch till December 2023.
- The Ujala has resulted in a reduction of 3.87 crore tonnes of CO_2 per year since its launch till December 2023.
- The Ujjawala scheme has resulted in a 13% reduction in deaths due to air pollution.
- In 2018, WHO praised the Ujjawala scheme for its achievement in shifting households to clean energy.
- The Ujjawala scheme slashed CO_2 emissions by shifting from residential fuel burning, which used to contribute 58%.

WITH A RESOLUTE AIM, THE AMRIT SAROVAR SCHEME REVIVED 75 PONDS PER DISTRICT, CREATING A SYMPHONY OF REJUVENATION RESONATING ACROSS 50,000+ WATER BODIES.

AMRIT SAROVAR COMPRISES PONDS WITH MINIMUM 1 ACRE PONDAGE AND 10,000 CUBIC METERS WATER CAPACITY.

COMPLETION REACHED 68,500 SITES OUT OF THE 68,500 INITIATED BY DECEMBER 10, 2023.

SERVES VARIOUS NEEDS: IRRIGATION, FISHERIES, DUCK, FARMING, WATER CHESTNUT CULTIVATION, WATER TOURISM AND MORE.

69. Ponds Revived: Amrit Sarovar Scheme's Journey

In the vibrant tapestry of Azadi ka Amrit Mahotsav, the Amrit Sarovar scheme unfolded in August 2022 as a visionary initiative, intertwining dreams of a revitalised Bharat. With a resolute aim, it revived 75 ponds per district, creating a symphony of rejuvenation resonating across 50,000+ water bodies nationwide by August 2023. Surpassing expectations, this remarkable achievement in May 2023 not only reflects the government's steadfast commitment but also adds a vibrant stroke to the canvas of 'Viksit Bharat's' journey toward a secure and sustainable future, embracing the essence of 'Amrit Kaal'.

- Amrit Sarovar comprises ponds with a minimum one-acre pondage and 10,000 cubic metres of water capacity.
- In addition to the achieved target, completion reached 68,500 sites out of the 84,177, initiated by 10 December, 2023.
- Excavated soil was repurposed by MORTH and Ministry of Railways for infrastructure projects.
- Vital for rainwater catchment, minimising of runoff carried out on a large scale.
- Serves various needs: irrigation, fisheries, duck farming, water chestnut cultivation, water tourism and more.

WIND ENERGY GENERATION HAS INCREASED 18X, REACHING 44.2 GW SINCE 2014, SECURING THE FOURTH GLOBAL POSITION AS OF NOVEMBER 2023.
INDIA PROUDLY EMERGES AS THE WORLD'S THIRD-LARGEST PRODUCER OF RENEWABLE ENERGY.
INDIA'S SOLAR POWER CAPACITY HAS SOARED 25X TO 72.01 GW SINCE 2014, RANKING THIRD GLOBALLY AS OF NOVEMBER 2023.

70. Renewable Bharat: A Sustainable Powerhouse

In the age of 'Amrit Kaal', 'Viksit Bharat' embarks on a transformative journey towards sustainability, unveiling an avant-garde renewable energy infrastructure. Nurtured by progressive government policies, this initiative harnesses the vitality of solar, wind and other eco-friendly sources, illuminating a vibrant future. It signifies Bharat's unwavering commitment to a thriving green tomorrow. With an ambitious target of 450 GW by 2030 – comprising 280 GW solar, 140 GW wind, and 10 GW bioenergy (achieved in 2022) – Bharat proudly emerges as the world's third-largest producer of renewable energy, with 43% of its electrical capacity sourced from non-fossil fuel origins.

- India's solar power capacity has soared 25x to 72.01 GW since 2014, ranking third globally as of November 2023.
- Wind energy generation has increased 18x, reaching 44.2 GW since 2014, securing the fourth global position as of November 2023.
- Biomass energy production sees a remarkable 131% rise, reaching 10.8 GW since 2014, as of November 2023.
- Non-fossil fuel energy generation in Bharat totals 179.8 GW, with hydropower at 46.8 GW, marking an 18.9% increase since 2014 as of November 2023.
- Achievements include 141.33 MW installed solar capacity, 2.78 lakh standalone solar pumps and 2,700 feeder-level solarisations under PM KUSUM, as of November 2023.

□

SKILL DEVELOPMENT CENTRE
HOMESTAY
Welcome

71. Borderland Prosperity: Vibrant Village Programme

This visionary programme creates a vibrant canvas of rural transformation, fostering livelihoods through tourism, cultural heritage and skill development. It cultivates cooperative societies, nurturing fields of agriculture and the healing touch of medicinal plants. Connecting forgotten villages with roads stitches together the fabric of progress. In borderland villages, operating within 0-10 kms from the International Boundary in 16 states and two UTs along land borders, it stands as a guardian, weaving socio-economic vibrancy. This initiative will boost tourism, generate employment, enhance skills and ensure that benefits reach the last mile. It's an artistic brush painting strokes of growth and an instrumental symphony enhancing national security during the 'Amrit Kaal'.

- The scheme aims to reverse the out-migration of people from border villages by creating opportunities for the locals.
- 2,967 villages in 46 border blocks of 19 districts in four states and one UT are identified under this programme.
- 17 border villages to be developed as tourist destinations. Homestays will be constructed under Deen Dayal Upadhyay Grih Awas Yojana.
- ₹2,500 crores will be spent exclusively on the creation of road infrastructure out of the total budget.
- Construction of 1,022-km-long roads in Arunachal Pradesh approved under the Vibrant Village programme in January 2024.

Rurban mission paints a vibrant future,
building a connected, prosperous and
inclusive rural india.

72. Vibrant Hues of Rurban Transformation: SPMRM

Forget stark divides, India's heartland thrums with a new rhythm – the Rurban Mission. The Rurban Mission, initiated in 2016, transcends development. It's a vibrant metamorphosis, harmonising rural and urban essence. The Syama Prasad Mookerji Rurban Mission envisions clusters preserving rural community life while embracing urban facilities. A 'Rurban cluster' comprises geographically contiguous villages, destined to reach 500 by 2025 and fostering thriving communities. This mission blurs stark divides, setting a new rhythm in India's heartland, emphasising equity, inclusiveness and a holistic blend of rural-urban attributes. It's not just a scheme; it's a dynamic blueprint igniting transformative change during the 'Amrit Kaal'.

- Rurban areas refer to a cluster of 15-20 contiguous villages having about 30 to 40 lakh population as per SPMRM.
- A total of 298 rurban clusters are approved out of 300 by 2022-23 at an expenditure of over ₹18,000 crores.
- Critical gap funding is provided to develop urban amenities in villages to develop rurban clusters.
- Agri-processing services, education and digital literacy, solid and liquid waste management and street lights are some of the facilities that are developed.
- Skill development, organic farming, renewables will minimise carbon footprint and thriving eco-future will empower rurban clusters.

Drone surveys in 2.88+ villages
Increased tax revenue
1 lakh common resources mapped in 2023
1.63+ crore property cards distributed.
PROPERTY CARD

74. GIS for Progress: SWAMITVA Mapping Rural India

Launched in 2021, the SWAMITVA scheme by the Government of India revolutionises rural land ownership. Using advanced technology, it maps and records individual and community land rights, addressing the historic challenge of undocumented holdings. This initiative ensures accurate land records for rural planning, reduces property disputes and empowers citizens by enabling property use for loans. It also aids property tax determination, enhances survey infrastructure and supports better-quality Gram Panchayat Development Plans through GIS maps. Beyond paperwork, formal recognition through SWAMITVA unlocks economic and social transformations, reshaping the landscape of rural India.

- 2.88+ lakh villages covered by drone surveys as of December 2023, creating a comprehensive digital land record database.
- 1.63+ crore property cards distributed as of December, boosting rural credit access.
- One lakh common resources mapped in 2023, empowering communities to protect forests and water bodies. Projections aim for 3 lakh resources mapped by 2025.
- Maps generated under the SVAMITVA scheme are geo-referenced maps capturing digital images of properties in rural populated areas.
- CORS monumentation was done at 1,018 sites and 903 CORS integrated with the control centre as of December 2023.

MINI
ATM

75. Doorstep Banking Serenade: Indian Post Payment Bank

In the symphony of financial innovation, the India Post Payments Bank (IPPB) emerges as a virtuoso, playing a transformative melody since its inception in 2017. IPPB envisions bringing the rhythm of banking to the doorsteps of millions, turning mundane transactions into a harmonious experience. Picture this: a doorstep adorned with financial possibilities. Open an account, transfer funds, dance with deposits, or serenade your bills – all orchestrated by IPPB's Doorstep Banking Services. It's not just banking; it's a lyrical journey where every note resonates with the heartbeat of financial accessibility in the 'Amrit Kaal'.

- IPPB is available at 1.55+ lakh post offices across the country out of which 1.36+ lakh are in rural areas by 2023.
- Over 3 lakh postmen as *grameen dak sevaks* are enabling the smooth functioning of IPPB even in the remotest areas with smartphones and digital biometric devices as of 2023.
- It generated a net profit of ₹20.16 crore during the financial year 2022-23.
- A growth of 66.12% in overall revenue was witnessed, which surpassed an increase in overall operating costs of 17.36%, showcasing a customer-centric and cost-effective banking model.
- 6.63+ crore IPPB accounts opened by the end of 2022-23 out of which 78% are from rural areas.

□

INFRA NATION
EXPRESSWAYS
ATAL TUNNEL
AIRPORTS
CHENAB BRIDGE
Anshul Gupta

Section-16

Infra Nation

"Infrastructure development is the driving force of the country's economy. PM Gati Shakti Master Plan is a critical tool that integrates economic and infrastructural planning with development. The speed and scale of infrastructure development are matching with the aspirations of 140 crore Indians."

—Prime Minister Shri Narendra Modi

(Post Budget Webinar on 04.03.2023 and Vande Bharat Flag-off, New Delhi on 24.09.2023)

HIGHWAYS
91,287 Kms
1,46,145 Kms
EXPRESSWAYS
1,004 Kms
5,145 KMs
RURAL ROADS
3.8LAKH KMS
7.4LAKH KMS
2014 2023
2014 2023
2014 2023
Anshul Gupta

76. Pavements to Prosperity: Bharatmala Symphony

Imagine Bharat rewired, connected by threads of asphalt, steel and concrete. No longer are megacities distant islands, nor are villages isolated whispers. This is the future woven by Bharatmala, India's ₹10.63 lakh crore tapestry of highways, economic corridors, border roads, coastal roads, expressways, tunnels and bridges, stretching over 83,677 kms. Revving from 12 to 37 kms/day (2014-23), 5000+ kms of border roads constructed since 2017 and 43,800+ kms of national highway being built as of December 2023, roads pave 'Viksit Bharat's' pavements to prosperity.

- 14,783 kms of highways completed as of October 2023 out of 34,800 kms approved under Phase 1 of the Bharatmala project in 2017.
- The length of national highways increased from 91,287 kms in 2014 to 1,46,145 kms in October 2023.
- The length of expressways has increased from 1,004 kms in 2014 to 5,145 kms by November 2023.
- Since 2014, the rural road connectivity has increased from 3.8 lakh kms to 7.4 lakh kms, ensuring better quality by August 2023.
- The average waiting time at toll plazas has reduced from 734 seconds to 47 seconds and it will soon be 30 seconds.

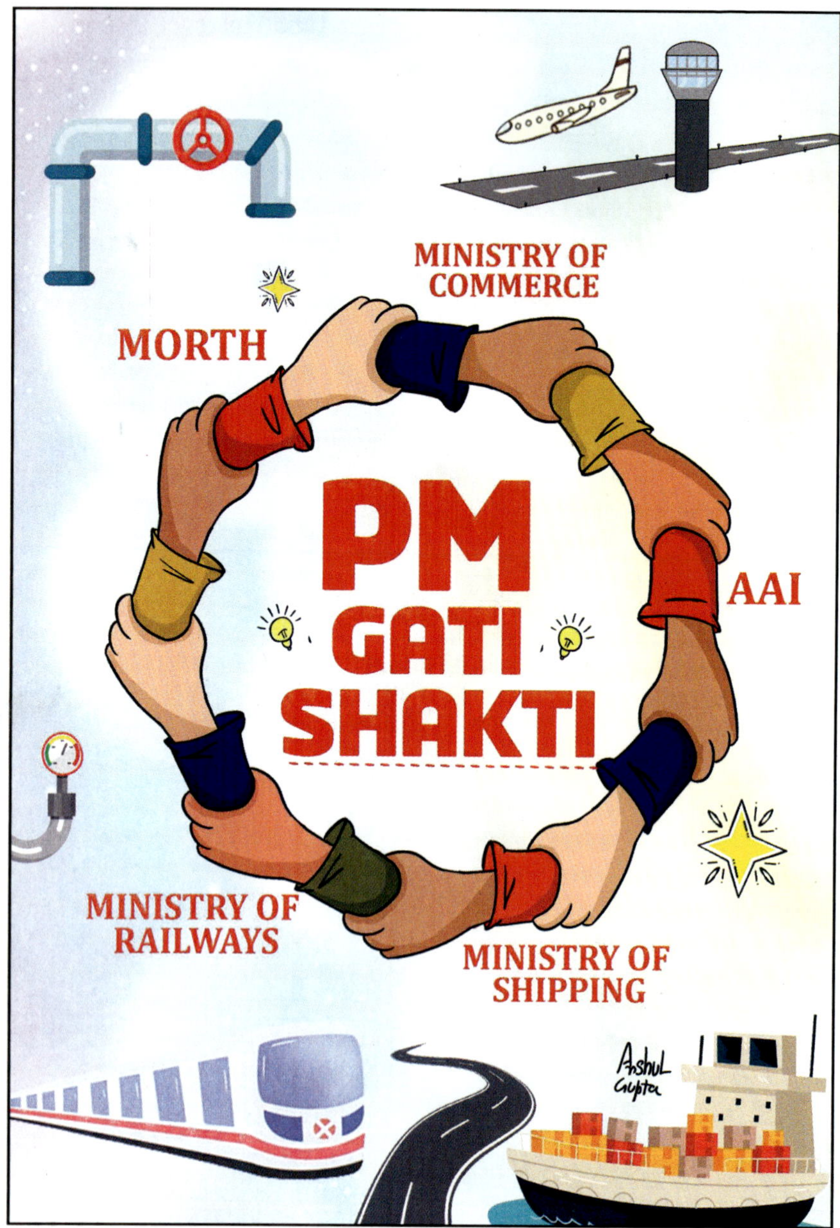
MINISTRY OF COMMERCE
MORTH
PM GATI SHAKTI
AAI
MINISTRY OF RAILWAYS
MINISTRY OF SHIPPING
Anshul Gupta

77. PM Gati Shakti: India's Infrastructure Symphony

India's ambitious Gatishakti, a $1.1 trillion symphony of infrastructure, orchestrates a future defined by speed, efficiency and a seamless flow of goods and people. This Master Plan, launched in 2021, transcends mere roads and bridges, weaving a multi-modal tapestry of highways, railways, waterways and airports, all singing in harmony. PM Gati Shakti, a digital master planning tool for 'Viksit Bharat', is integrating infrastructural schemes across economic zones via dynamic GIS mapping capable of integrating hundreds of data layers. It operates on pillars of comprehensiveness, prioritisation, optimisation, synchronisation, analytical and dynamic principles with a target of achieving a $20 trillion economy by 2040 in 'Amrit Kaal'.

- PM Gati Shakti aims to cut logistical costs to 9% of GDP by 2025, saving ₹10 lakh crore yearly, down from 13-14%.
- Goals include a 20% reduction in project delays, 30% lower material costs and a 15% increase in transparency by 2025.
- Two lakh kms of highways, 220 new airports and 1,759 MMTPA total cargo capacity by 2025.
- 1,600 million tonnes of total cargo, 34,500 kms of pipelines and 4.54+ lakh circuit kms by 2025.
- PM Gati Shakti outlines 1,300 projects across ministries as discussed in the December 2023 61st National Planning Group meeting.

AIRPORT 2014-74 | 2023-149
UDAN
LOCAL GOODS
Ashul Gupta

78. UDAN: Bharat Takes Off on a Connectivity Revolution

Forget long, dusty roads and cramped bus journeys. India's audacious regional connectivity scheme, UDAN (*Ude Desh ka Aam Nagrik*) has transformed regional air travel from a distant dream to a daily reality. This ambitious initiative, launched in 2016, isn't just connecting far-flung towns; it's weaving a web of opportunity, transforming lives and propelling Bharat towards a sky-high future. From 74 in 2014 to 149 in November 2023, the country saw a surge in airports, heliports and water aerodromes. Aiming for 42 crore air travellers by 2030, 180 RCS airports, 25 water aerodromes and 40 helipads are identified. UDAN has revolutionised regional air travel, making flying affordable and accessible for millions.

- 76 airports operationalised, stitching together remote regions across 30 states by November 2023.
- 517 RCS routes made operational as of November 2023, bridging underserved towns with major hubs.
- UDAN sets ₹2500 airfare for a one-hour fixed-wing or half-hour helicopter journey covering 500 kms, while the country aims for 15 dual airport cities in Bharat by 2040.
- Meghalaya farmers reach city markets with fresh produce; village students access higher education thanks to UDAN-enabled air routes.
- *Growth engine*: Projected market size of ₹85,000 crores by 2025, creating 12 lakh new jobs in aviation and tourism.

Anshul Gupta
2013
Metro rail network 250 km
2023
Metro rail network 860 km

80. Metro Rails: Enhancing Urban Mobility

Since 2014, Bharat has witnessed a paradigm shift in urban transport, driven by the vision of 'Viksit Bharat'. The Metro rail network, a key component, propels economic growth and modern urbanisation. With a nearly threefold increase in operational lines, it markedly alleviates congestion, serving almost one crore passengers daily, as of 2023. Currently the world's third largest, it's on track to surpass the USA's Metro network by 2025-26. The ambitious goal is to extend the network to 5,000 kms across 100 cities by 2047, shaping a dynamic and efficient urban infrastructure for the new Bharat in 'Amrit Kaal'.

- The Metro rail network has increased from less than 250 kms in 2014 to 860 kms by early 2023.
- More than 980 kms of the Metro network are currently under construction in 27 cities, as of October 2023.
- The monthly average of Metro lines has increased from 0.68 km in 2014 to 5.6 kms as of April 2023.
- The 520-metre-long tunnel connecting Howrah and Kolkata is India's first underwater Metro tunnel.
- India's first RRTS 'Namo Bharat' between Delhi–Ghaziabad – Meerut was inaugurated in October 2023 out of eight routes identified in NCR.

□

SMART SHIKSHA
PM SHRI
DISHA
SWAYAM
EDUCATION POLICY 2020
माँ
తల్లి
মা
માતા
Anshul Gupta

Section-17

Smart Shiksha

"Through the New Education Policy, the country is for the first time preparing an education system which is forward-looking and futuristic."

—Prime Minister Shri Narendra Modi
(75th Amrut Mahotsav, Shree Swaminarayan Gurukul, Rajkot on 22.12.2022)

100% GER in preschool to secondary education by 2030 and in higher education to 50% by 2035, up from 26.3% in 2018.
Health and wellness
Conciousness studies
Traditional knowledge in mathematics
Astronomy
Indian knowledge system
Traditional medicines, yoga,, vedas
Ancient stuctures and design
Preserving art, culture and tradition
' PARAKH', 'NISHTHA', 'SPARC', 'MERU'AND 'GIAN'.
10+2
5+3+3+4
বাংলা
اردو
मराठी
हिन्दी
ਪੰਜਾਬੀ
ଓଡ଼ିଆ

81. NEP 2020: Education Revolution Unleashed

The British-imposed education system in Bharat disrupted traditional learning, fostering illiteracy and socio-economic disparities. The

National Education Policy 2020 transcends a mere policy; it scripts the destiny of the 'Amrit Peedhi' in the 'Amrit Kaal', revolutionising education from schools to universities. Featuring the innovative 5+3+3+4 curricular structure, initiatives like 'PARAKH', 'NISHTHA', 'SPARC', 'MERU' and 'GIAN,' emphasis on multilingual education, universal schooling access and advocating a substantial increase in public investment to 6% of GDP, NEP 2020 establishes a sturdy foundation for a developed India, anchored in the pillars of quality, equity, accessibility and affordability.

- It aims for 100% GER in preschool to secondary education by 2030 and in higher education to 50% by 2035, up from 26.3% in 2018.
- It recommends using the mother tongue, local language till Grade 5, ideally extending to Grade 8 and beyond as a medium of instruction.
- It recommends the incorporation of the Indian Knowledge System (IKS) into the curriculum at all levels of education.
- It enables flexible, multidisciplinary higher education with multiple entry/exit options.
- It encourages top global universities to set up in Bharat and encourages Indian institutes to establish campuses abroad.

PM SHRI
14500 schools to be developed.

83. PM SHRI: Transforming Education Landscape

Pioneering a visionary education model for 'Viksit Bharat', the Cabinet greenlit Pradhan Mantri Schools for Rising India (PM SHRI) in 2022, is an innovative scheme, aligned with the National Education Policy (NEP) 2020. It seeks to be an exemplar, showcasing advanced infrastructure, inventive pedagogy, and technology integration. As these model schools evolve, they are poised to not only implement NEP 2020 but also provide leadership to neighbouring educational institutions. PM SHRI is dedicated to delivering qualitative and innovative education, employing a modern, transformative and holistic approach to nurture 21st-century skills.

- PM SHRI unveils a transformative school scheme with a ₹27,360 crore project cost spanning five years (2022-23 to 2026-27).
- Over 14,500 schools nationwide to become PM SHRI schools, showcasing all aspects of NEP 2020.
- PM SHRI integrates skills with local industries, promoting internships, entrepreneurship and tailored curriculum for impactful development.
- PM SHRI schools will be enabled with ICT, smart classrooms and digital libraries for using digital pedagogy.
- *First phase of PM SHRI schools*: 6,207 selected from 27 states/UTs, including KVS/NVS, benefiting over 35 lakh students as of December 2023.

E-Vidya Portals
• SWAYAM
• NDLI
• SATHEE
• NDEAR
• DIKSHA
FREE ONLINE EDUCATION
swayam

84. PM e-Vidya: Unlocking Digital Learning

In the era of digital enlightenment, Bharat experiences a profound learning metamorphosis through PM e-Vidya. Beyond conventional classrooms, education takes flight on vibrant wings, embodied by three portals: SWAYAM, NDLI, SATHEE, NDEAR and DIKSHA. With 200 PM e-Vidya DTH TV channels, states offer multilingual supplementary education for Grades 1-12. These platforms transcend information repositories, acting as catalysts for up-skilling, cultural immersion and teacher empowerment. Explore how these portals fuel a knowledge renaissance in the 'Amrit Kaal', ushering in an empowering wave for learners and educators in my book.

- SWAYAM: 3.5 crore+ enrolments in 6,945+ free courses with 135 universities by December 2023.
- NDLI: 80 million+ visitors exploring 5.4 million+ digitised books, fostering cultural understanding.
- DIKSHA: 17 crores+ enrolments, 15,600+ courses and 5.3 billion learning sessions since the December 2023 launch.
- Special e-content for the visually and hearing impaired on DAISY and in sign language on the NIOS website/ YouTube.
- *NDEAR*: Unified digital infrastructure with 1,500+ micro courses, 5B+ sessions, 12B+ QR codes and 20K+ participants. Ongoing improvements: 15K+.

7 IITs
7 IIMs
15 AIIMs

85. Vibrant Academia: India's Global Footprint

India's higher education advances global competitiveness, emphasising innovation and skills. Cutting-edge research facilities, technology integration and interdisciplinary studies propel institutions worldwide. Government initiatives under 'Viksit Bharat' promote international collaborations, offering diverse perspectives. Learner-centric measures like NCrF, National Higher Education Qualification Framework, Academic Bank of Credit and multiple entry/exit foster education adaptability. Universities increased from 723 in 2014 to 1,113 in 2023. 148 Indian universities featured in the QS World University List Asia 2024. Encouraging entrepreneurship, critical thinking and a global mindset, Bharat shapes graduates for an interconnected world, boosting economic growth and solidifying a strong global academic presence.

- 41 universities from Bharat in 2023 QS World Rankings List compared to just 12 in 2014.
- Study in India portal is going to be a pivotal step in making Bharat a preferred destination for higher education.
- 5,298 colleges have been built in the last nine years (up from 38,498 in 2014 to 43,796 in 2023).
- Seven new IITs, seven new IIMs and 15 new AIIMS were set up in 2014 by 2023.
- JEE, NEET, CUET in 13 languages; 100 UG books in 12 languages; 20 tech books in Indian languages for first-year students, enhancing linguistic inclusivity in higher education.

□

SWASTHA VITAL

Ashul Gupta

Section-18

Swastha Vital

"True progress is people-centric. No matter how many advances are made in medical science, access must be assured to the last person at the last mile."

—Prime Minister Shri Narendra Modi

(6th Edition of One Health One Earth AHCI 2023 on 26.04.2023)

10,000th Jan Aushadhi Kendra inaugurated at AIIMS, Deodhar in nov 2023
PRADHAN MANTRI
BHARTIYA JAN AUSHADHI KENDRA
Generic Medical Store
High Quality Cheaper Medicines
50-90% discount

86. Jan Aushadi: Affordable Care for Everyone

In a transformative leap for Indian healthcare, the Pradhan Mantri Bharatiya Jan Aushadhi Pariyojana (PMB-JAP) has evolved into a beacon of accessible, high-quality generic medicines. Launched in 2015, this game-changer achieved a monumental milestone in 2023, selling medicines worth ₹1000 crores. With Jan Aushadhi Kendras spanning 785 districts, it has saved a remarkable ₹5,000 crore. This historic initiative propels Bharat towards the vision of 'Viksit Bharat', ensuring affordable and quality healthcare for all.

- 1965 generic medicines and 293 surgical products were added to the basket as of November 2023.
- Since 2014, ₹25000 crore has been saved through this *pariyojana* by December 2023.
- *Network expansion*: 10,000+ *kendras* serving 1.2 crore daily as of November 2023, aiming for 12,000 by March 2024.
- 1.2 lakh jobs through franchises, empowering communities as of November 2023.
- 120+ labs ensure safe, effective medicines at Jan Aushadhi Kendras.
- 16.7+ crore citizens served with free telemedicine through the e-sanjeevani scheme as of October 2023.

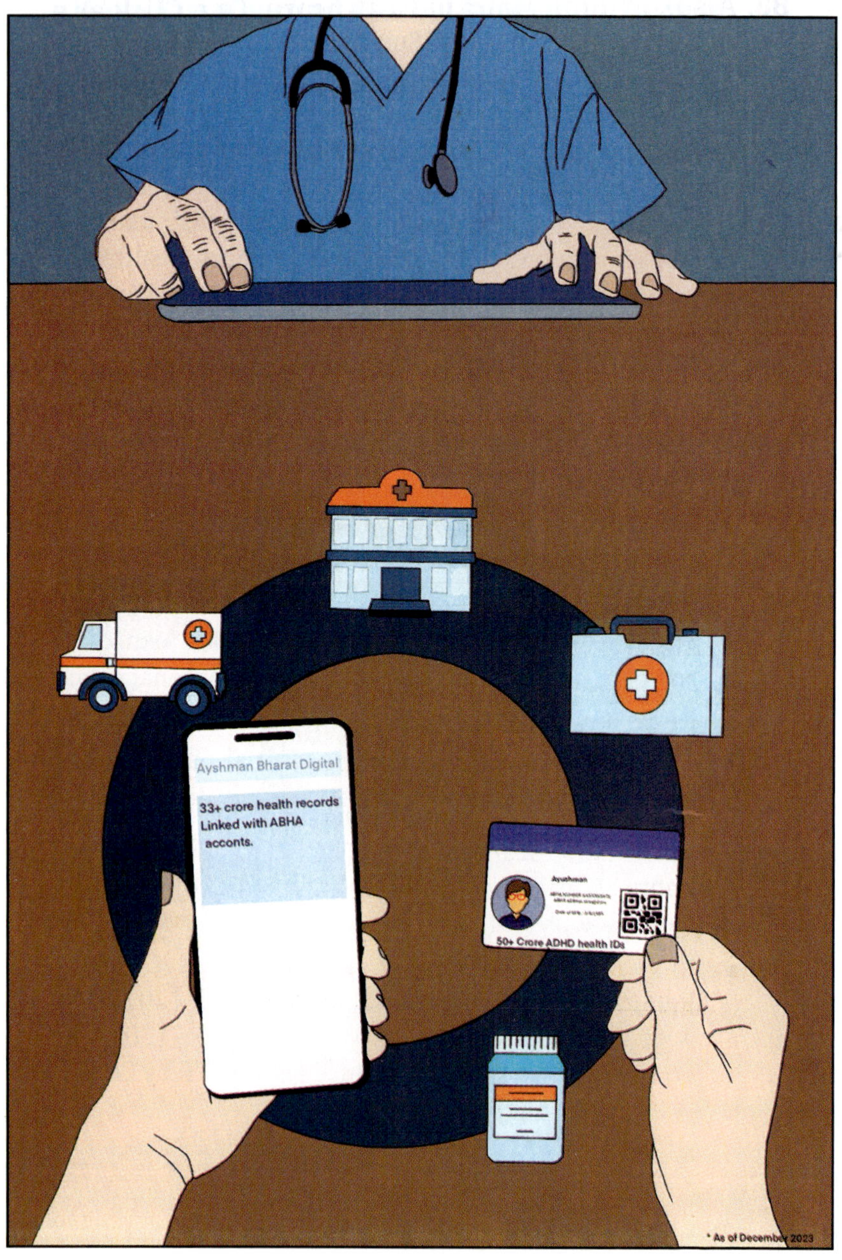
Ayshman Bharat Digital
33+ crore health records Linked with ABHA acconts.
Ayushman
50+ Crore ADHD health IDs
* As of December 2023

88. ABDHM: Empowering Healthcare, One Click at a Time

Aayushman Bharat, through the Digital Health Mission (ABDM), envisions healthcare as a trusted companion, emphasising seamless management by eliminating data silos. With an outlay of ₹1600 crore for five years (21-22 to 25-26), ABDM leverages open, interoperable, standards-based digital systems. Prioritising security, confidentiality and privacy, it pioneers comprehensive and secure healthcare access. This initiative heralds a new era, developing the backbone for integrated digital health infrastructure and bridging gaps among stakeholders through digital highways. Aiming for 'Viksit Bharat', ABDM sets the stage for efficient, accessible and inclusive healthcare.

- 33+ crore health records linked with ABHA accounts of patients with 50+ lakh mobile app downloads by December 2023.
- ABDM enables 30 lakh teleconsultations (by October 2023), bridging geographical gaps.
- 1.5 crore patients have used ABHA-based instant OPD registration service by December 2023.
- Over 2.5+ lakh healthcare facilities and 2.6+ lakh healthcare professionals (by December 2023) embrace ABDM, streamlining processes with digitised prescriptions and diagnostics.
- 50 crore individuals have ABHA numbers as their unique health IDs by December 2023.

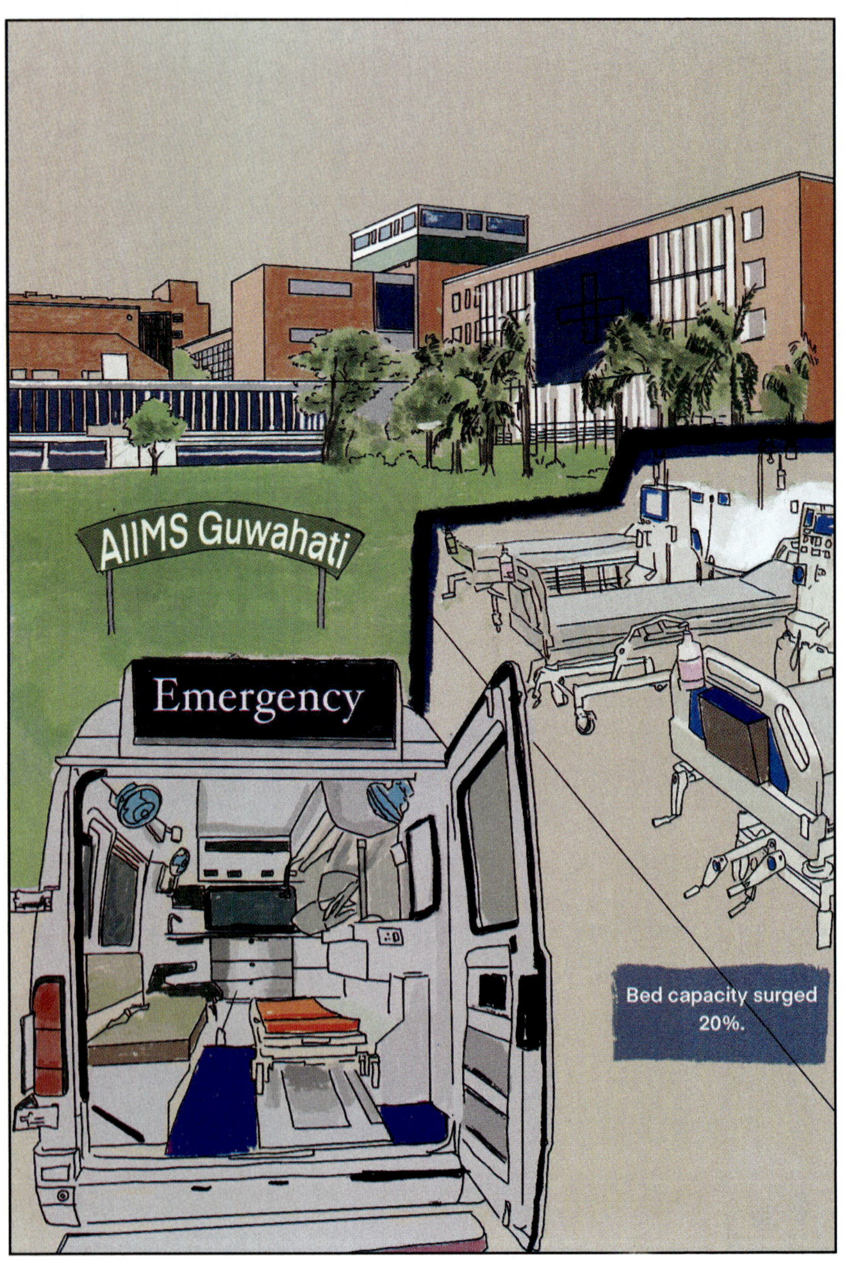
AIIMS Guwahati
Emergency
Bed capacity surged 20%.

89. Ayushman Bharat: Expanding Healthcare Infra

India's healthcare landscape undergoes a robust transformation as the government amplifies medical infrastructure, doubling the budget from 2014 to 2023. The Prime Minister's launch of the PM-Ayushman Bharat Health Infrastructure Mission (PM-ABHIM) allocates ₹ 64,180 crore for six years from 2021. This mission strategically focuses on bolstering health system capacities at all care levels – primary, secondary and tertiary. With an eye on effective pandemic/ disaster response, PM-ABHIM aims to fortify the healthcare framework, contributing to a resilient and developed India. This financial commitment signals a significant leap towards a robust healthcare ecosystem, aligning with the vision of 'Viksit Bharat'.

- 1.63 lakh Ayushman Mandirs operational by December 2023, including 1.22+ lakh SHCs and 23,600+ PHCs.
- This scheme allocates ₹ 19,064.80 crores for Critical Care Hospitals in 602 districts.
- 100+ revamped hospitals with modern facilities and specialists, increasing bed capacity by 20%.
- Patient wait times reduced by 25% and specialist consultations increased by 30% as compared to pre-2014.
- Since 2014, 275 new medical colleges by April 2023, boosting MBBS seats by 97% and post-graduate seats by 110%, addressing personnel shortage.

Over 10 crore beneficiaries served under POSHAN Abhiyan.
5.06 crore children and 1.25 crore pregnant women since 2014 under mission Indradhanush.

90. Child Health Triumph: POSHAN and Indradhanush

The government's dual initiatives, POSHAN Abhiyan and Mission Indradhanush focus on children's health. POSHAN Abhiyan combats malnutrition by prioritising the first 1,000 days, ensuring proper nutrition and health education. Simultaneously, Mission Indradhanush aims for full immunisation coverage, targeting unvaccinated and partially vaccinated children. Together, these efforts epitomise the government's comprehensive strategy to enhance child health, addressing both malnutrition and immunisation gaps. These initiatives collectively pave the way for a healthier and more resilient 'Amrit Peedhi' in 'Viksit Bharat'.

- Over 10 crore beneficiaries served under POSHAN Abhiyan as of December 2023.
- States/UTs conducted 90+ crore awareness activities during 11 Poshan Maahs, fostering community engagement for nutrition in September and March-April.
- Poshan Tracker uses technology to identify child malnutrition and track nutrition service delivery in real time.
- Mission Indradhanush has vaccinated 5.06 crore children and 1.25 crore pregnant women since 2014.
- The communication strategy featured a 360-degree approach, addressing vaccine hesitancy and engaging local influencers and leaders.

□

LEGAL OVERHAUL

Section-19

Legal Overhaul

"Like ease of doing business and ease of living, ease of justice is equally important in 'Amrit Yatra' of the country."

—Prime Minister Shri Narendra Modi

(First All India District Legal Services Authorities Meet on 30.07.2022)

TELE-LAW
• Tele-Law available on 2,50,000 CSCs
• 6.02 crore cases advised
NYAYA ADALAT
• implemented in 7 blocks of Assam and Jammu & Kashmir
• ADR (Alternate Dispute Resolution)
NYAYA BANDHU
• 10,629 advocates registered
• 22 high courts established Pro Bono Panels
Anshul Gupta

91. Nyaya Bandhu and Tele-Law: Legal Innovations

In the symphony of legal innovation, tele-law orchestrates access with a front-office legal ensemble, harmonising justice delivery. Nyaya Bandhu, a legal altruist, connects benevolent lawyers with seekers, a melody of assistance resonating for those in need. This sonnet of inclusivity bridges legal divides, serenading individuals and organisations. As the government choreographs 'Nari Adalat' under Mission Shakti, it's a ballet of change – phases addressing domestic discord, property poignancy and patriarchal challenges. A legal odyssey, 'Viksit Bharat' unfolds with Alternative Dispute Resolution, crafting a nation where justice harmonises with every heartbeat.

- Phase 1 of the 'Nari Adalat' implementation spans seven blocks in Assam and two aspirational districts in J&K from 2023.
- Nyaya Bandhu sees 10,629 advocates registered across 24 state bar councils and 89 law schools in the Pro Bono club scheme by November 2023.
- 22 high courts establish Pro Bono panels; 1,354 advocates to be enrolled under the Nyaya Bandhu initiative by November 2024.
- Tele-Law to reach 2,50,000 CSCs across 28 states and eight UTs via video conferencing/telephone.
- Over 6.02 crore cases advised out of 6.09 crore cases registered under the Tele-Law initiative.

Budget Layout Phase 3:2023-27-INR 7210 Crore
857 eSewa kendra
Anshul Gupta

92. Smart Justice: E-Courts Mission Unveiled

The E-Courts Mission Mode Project, a catalyst for technological strides in justice, aims to make legal processes efficient, transparent and citizen-centric. Envisioned to enhance judicial productivity, Phase-III, a four-year Central Sector Scheme from 2023, focuses on a unified, paperless interface. This project aligns with the Litigant's Charter, automating processes, ensuring accessibility and making justice in 'Viksit Bharat' affordable, reliable and transparent. Sanctioned in 2015, the initiative expands hardware provisions in Phase II, covering courts comprehensively. The Union Cabinet's approval underscores a commitment to a seamless, digital justice ecosystem connecting courts, litigants and stakeholders.

- A total budget outlay for Phase III spanning four years from 2023 is ₹7210 crores.
- Phase II of the project started in 2015 under which 18,735 district and subordinate courts have been computerised by March 2023.
- A new e-filing system (version 3.0) has been rolled out for electronic filing of legal papers with upgraded features in February 2023.
- Leveraging AI and its subsets, including ML, OCR and NLP, creates a smart ecosystem, enhancing user experience for seamless interaction.
- 857 E-Sewa Kendras bridge the tech gap, ensuring all citizens access to judicial services inclusively at district courts nationwide as of December 2023.

-Dedicated commercial court below district level : 758
-Dedicated commercial court at district judge level : 379
-Commercial appellate court at district judge level : 494

93. Commercial Courts Act: Business-friendly Justice

The government, aiming to position Bharat as a premier investment hub, prioritises business-friendly laws like the Commercial Courts Act, of 2015. This underscores a commitment to foster an investment-friendly environment. Simultaneously, judicial reforms entail a collaborative effort involving the judiciary and legislature to expedite justice, emphasising Alternative Dispute Resolution. The Commercial Courts Act, 2015 and its 2018 amendment introduce Pre-Institution Mediation and Settlement for commercial disputes, with features like appellate and district-level commercial courts. This multifaceted approach not only streamlines dispute resolution, but also enhances the ease of doing business, aligning with the vision of 'Viksit Bharat'.

- Amendment Act reduces commercial dispute threshold from one crore to three lakhs for broader court jurisdiction.
- 758 commercial courts below the District Judge level empower state governments to establish as of May 2023.
- Allows appeals from commercial courts to 379 Commercial Appellate Courts at the District Judge level as of May 2023.
- 494 dedicated commercial courts existed as of May 2023 at the District Judge level.
- Average trial and judgment time for a commercial case reduced from 1,095 days to 306 days.

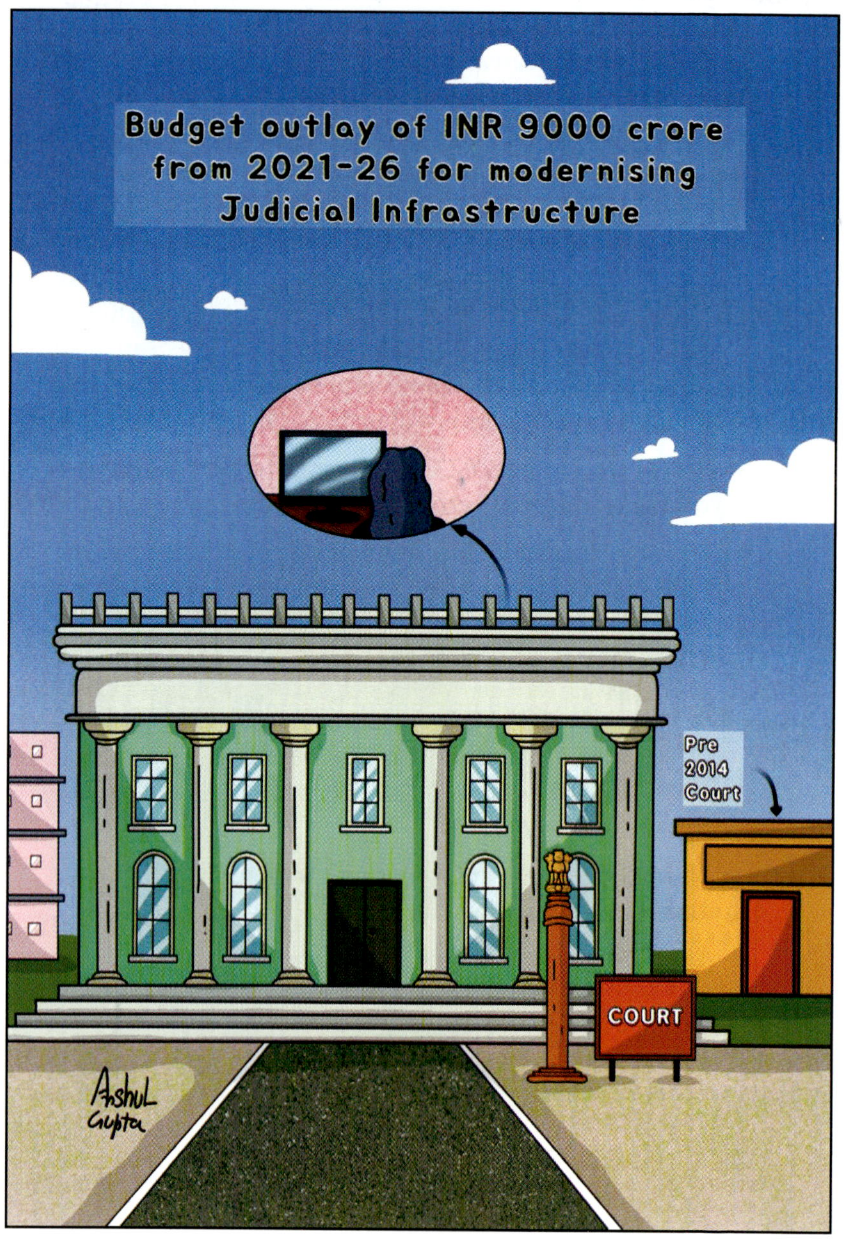
Budget outlay of INR 9000 crore from 2021-26 for modernising Judicial Infrastructure
Pre 2014 Court
COURT
Anshul Gupta

95. Judicial Facelift: Visionary Infrastructure Development

In a visionary stride towards 'Viksit Bharat', the Union Cabinet had greenlit the continued Centrally Sponsored Scheme (CSS) for judiciary infrastructure development for five years from 2021. Recognising the persistent challenges, the initiative addresses rented or dilapidated court premises and inadequate residential facilities for judicial officers. This commitment aligns with the government's sensitivity to judicial infrastructure, aiming for well-equipped courts and residences. By enhancing resources for states, this CSS fuels the construction of modern court buildings, residential quarters, lawyer halls and digital facilities – vital steps in ensuring easy access, timely justice and a technologically inclusive legal landscape for all.

- A substantial budget of ₹9,000 crore, with a significant Central share of ₹5,357 crore, had been allocated from 2021 to 2026.
- It involves the construction of 3,800 court halls and 4,000 residential units for judicial officers in district and subordinate courts.
- It covers the development of 1,450 lawyer halls, 1,450 toilet complexes and 3,800 digital computer rooms.
- ₹50 crores for *gram nyayalayas*, providing recurring and non-recurring grants for five years in 2021.
- The government had sanctioned ₹5200 crores accounting for nearly 60% of the sanction made from 2014-2021.

□

CROP LIFT

Section-20

Crop Lift

"Our farmers are our 'annadatas'. When our farmers prosper, Bharat will prosper. Their confidence is the strength of the country."

—Prime Minister Shri Narendra Modi

(Twitter, 17.03.2017)

ONLINE TRADING
QUICK PAYMENTS
E-NAM SCHEME
ACCESS TO MORE MARKET
ACCURATE INFORMATION
1.76 CRORE FARMERS ENROLLED
1389 MANDIS
2.5 LAKH TRADERS ONBOARD
Ashul Gupta

96. e-NAM: Cultivating Prosperity in Agriculture

Since its inception in 2016, the e-NAM scheme has revolutionised agriculture, turning it from a conventional occupation into a dynamic realm of opportunities. This innovative platform integrates APMC *mandis* nationwide, establishing a unified electronic trading system. Its objective is to facilitate pan-Bharat trade in agricultural commodities by dismantling traditional barriers. The transparent auction process, rooted in produce quality, ensures improved price discovery. The efficiency of the National Agriculture Market is further heightened by timely online payments, contributing to the development of a 'Viksit Bharat' with smart *kisans* farmers) and fostering growth and prosperity in the sector.

- 1.76 crore farmers enrolled on e-NAM by November 2023.
- 1,389 *mandis* integrated from 23 states and 4 UTs as of November 2023.
- 3,366 FPOs and over 2.5 lakh traders onboarded the platform by November 2023.
- Total traded value exceeded ₹3 lakh crores on the platform by November 2023.
- Key outcomes include an enhanced supply chain, reduced wastage, a unified trading licence for Bharat and increased price share for farmers.

Aiming for 7.5 lakh hectares across 15,000 clusters by 2027, with a budget of INR 1584 crore.
Farmers adopting natural farming receive INR 15,000 per hectare support for three years.
National Mission on Natural Farming (NMNF) launches independently from 2023-24, expanding Bhartiya Prakritik Krishi Paddati (BPKP).
Farmer field schools train farmers for natural farming adoption.
NATURAL MISSION FOR
NATURAL FARMING
Targeting 15,000 Bhartiya Prakritik Kheti Bio -inputs Resource Centres by 2027.
Ashul Gupta

97. NMNF: Nurturing Natural Farming for a 'Viksit Bharat'

The perilous consequences of extensive pesticide use on the environment, health and biodiversity necessitate a critical transition to natural farming. The government's visionary National Mission on Natural Farming stands as a pivotal force in rejuvenating Indian agriculture. Through the promotion of chemical-free farming, it inspires farmers to adopt sustainable practices, catalysing the widespread embrace of natural farming techniques nationwide. The mission's innovative approach involves creating farmer clusters, each overseeing 50 hectares, fostering a sense of community and shared knowledge during the transformative 'Amrit Kaal' for the development of a resilient and progressive 'Viskit Bharat'.

- National Mission on Natural Farming (NMNF) launches independently from 2023-24, expanding Bhartiya Prakritik Krishi Paddati (BPKP).
- Aiming for 7.5 lakh hectares across 15,000 clusters by 2027, with a budget of ₹1,584 crores.
- Farmers adopting natural farming receive ₹15,000 per hectare support for three years.
- Farmer field schools train farmers for natural farming adoption.
- Targeting 15,000 Bhartiya Prakritik Kheti Bio-inputs Resource Centres by 2027.

National Productivity Council study affirms 8%-10% chemical fertilizer reduction with SHC.
Soil samples analyzed on 12 parameters in 10,000+ GIS-mapped government labs.
23 Crore Soil Health Cards distributed by August 2023, following soil sample testing
Detailed Soil Mapping at 1:10000 scale uses satellite data and field surveys in priority areas.
SOIL HEALTH CARD
Nation wide programme to improve soil health
Ashul Gupta

98. Fertile Future: Soil Health Card

As the world's second-largest agricultural producer, this nation stands at the forefront of global food security. The foundation for enduring farmer prosperity is fertile soil. Initiated in 2015 and subsequently integrated into the Rashtriya Krishi Vikas Yojana since 2022-23, the Soil Health Card, known as 'Soil Health & Fertility', targets an optimal NPK ratio of 4:2:1. This strategic move, aimed at curbing fertiliser overuse, has yielded positive results by reducing cultivation costs, augmenting farmer income and minimising dependency on chemical fertilisers. It represents a significant step towards both soil sustainability and farmer profitability in the transformative era of 'Amrit Kaal'.

- 23 crore Soil Health Cards distributed by August 2023, following soil sample testing.
- Soil samples analysed on 12 parameters in 10,000+ GIS-mapped government labs.
- SHC portal integrated with GIS since April 2023, automating soil testing.
- Detailed soil mapping at 1:10,000 scale uses satellite data and field surveys in priority areas.
- National Productivity Council study affirms 8-10% chemical fertiliser reduction with SHC.

The scheme supports farmers in covering agricultural expenses and adopting modern farming technologies.
100% Funding from government of india
As on November 2023, 11.27 crore farmers are beneficiaries of the PM-KISAN scheme.
Direct Income support of Rs. 6000 p.a for farmers in three equal installments of Rs. 2000 /-
BANK
PM Kisan Samman Nidhi
Anshul Gupta

99. Empowering Farmers with PM-KISAN

Unveiled in 2019, the PM-Kisan Samman Nidhi Yojana stands as a transformative force, steering Indian agriculture toward prosperity and sustainability, aligning with the 2047 vision of 'Viksit Bharat'. As the world's largest Direct Benefit Transfer scheme, this digital marvel empowers farmers. Operating as a Central Sector Scheme, PM-KISAN extends financial aid to cultivable landholding families, prioritising transparency. Leveraging farmer-centric digital infrastructure, the scheme eliminates middlemen, ensuring seamless and fair distribution of benefits to farmers nationwide. It emerges as a beacon of change, propelling India's agricultural landscape into a new era of growth and self-sufficiency.

- An annual amount of ₹6,000 is transferred in three equal instalments of ₹2,000 directly into the Aadhaar bank accounts of 11.27 crore farmers.
- Over ₹2.80 lakh crores has been disbursed to farmers since the scheme's launch, including the 15th instalment in November 2023.
- As of November 2023, 11.27 crore farmers are beneficiaries of the PM-KISAN scheme.
- The PM-KISAN AI Chatbot (Kisan e-Mitra) provides farmers with a one-stop solution for their grievances related to the scheme, even in regional languages.
- The scheme's financial assistance supports farmers in covering agricultural expenses, buying seeds and fertilisers and adopting modern farming technologies.

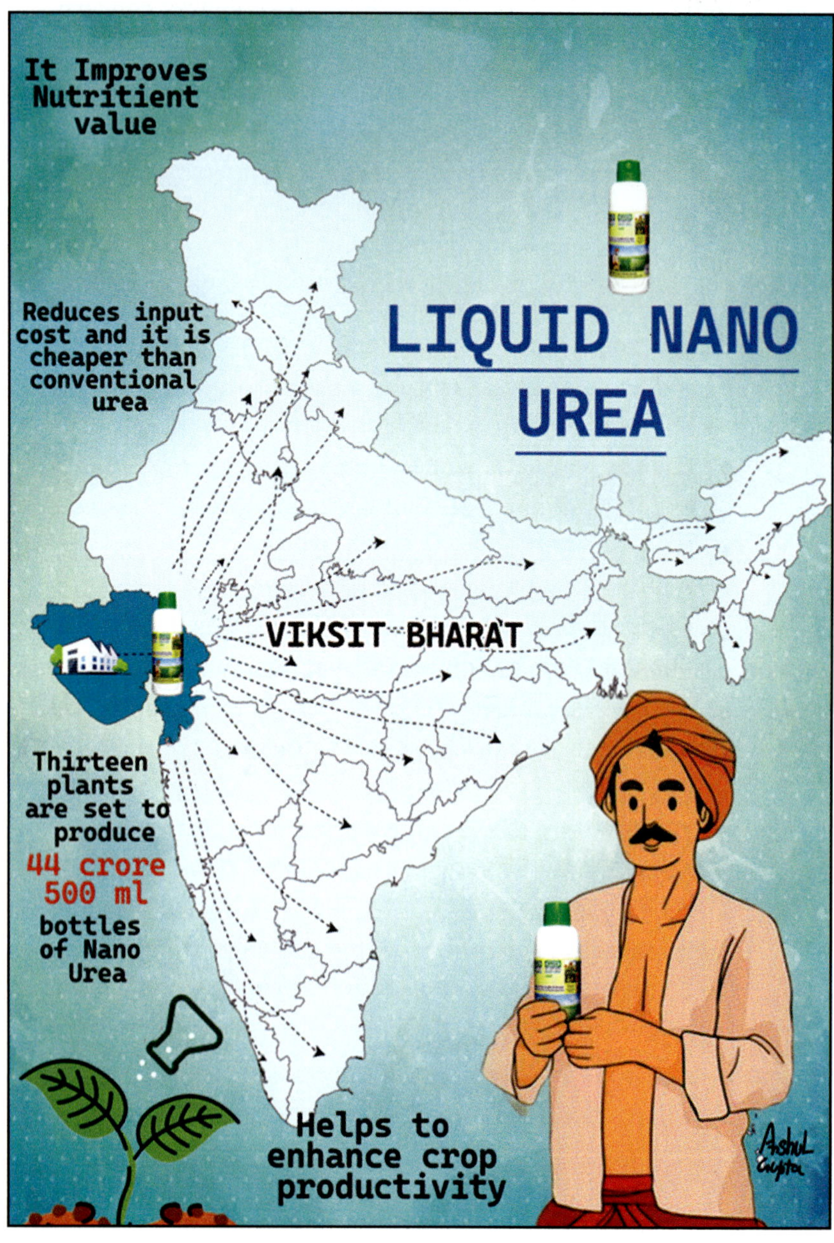
It Improves Nutritient value
LIQUID NANO UREA
Reduces input cost and it is cheaper than conventional urea
VIKSIT BHARAT
Thirteen plants are set to produce
44 crore 500 ml
bottles of Nano Urea
Helps to enhance crop productivity
Ashul Gupta

100. Liquid Nano-Urea Reshaping Fertiliser Dynamics

India, heavily reliant on imported urea, sparks concern, leading to pioneering government investment in world's first nano-urea production. Developed at Gujarat's Nano Biotechnology Research Centre, this liquid nitrogen alternative, in nanoparticle form, aligns with 'Atmanirbhar Bharat' and 'Atmanirbhar Krishi', proving cost-effective for farmers and cutting logistical expenses. With a vision for 'Viksit Bharat', the nation aims for complete urea import independence by 2025, revolutionising the fertiliser landscape. Nine plants are operational as of December 2023, launched in May 2022.

- Thirteen plants are set to produce 44 crore 500 ml bottles of nano-urea and DAP by 2025.
- Each 500 ml bottle of nano-urea and DAP replaces a 45 kg bag of traditional urea.
- Substituting 25% nano-urea for conventional urea by 2025 will save ₹15,000-20,000 annually in imports.
- Liquid nano-urea boasts an impressive efficiency of 85-90%, surpassing conventional urea's 25% efficiency.
- ICAR reports a 3-8% yield advantage through foliar application of nano-urea alongside the recommended dose of conventional urea.